# A Good Place To Be

A Leadership Guide for
Making Your Vision a Reality...
- *Within Your School*
- *Within Your Classroom*
- *Within Your Family*
- *Within Your Heart*

## Mary Curtis Aranha

PUBLISHING

DUDE PUBLISHING
A Division of
National Professional Resources, Inc.
Port Chester, New York

Aranha, Mary Curtis.
  A good place to be : a leadership guide for making
your vision a reality-- within your school, within your
classroom, within your family, within your heart / Mary
Curtis Aranha. -- 1st ed.
  p. cm.
  ISBN 1-887943-60-9

  1. Educational leadership. 2.School management and
organization. 3. School improvement programs.
I. Title

LB2806.A73 2002              371.2
                         QBI02-200177

Cover/Book Design & Production by Andrea Cerone, National Professional
Resources, Inc., Port Chester, NY

Dude Publishing
A Division of National Professional Resources, Inc.
25 South Regent Street
Port Chester, New York 10573
Toll free: (800) 453-7461
Phone: (914) 937-8879

Visit our Web site: www.nprinc.com

Printed in the United States of America

ISBN 1-887943-60-9

To my husband, Fred,

and to my children, India, Serese and Ivan.

In memory of my parents, James and Elizabeth Curtis.

# Also featuring the Author...

## VIDEO

### *Leadership: The Character Education Imperative*

No longer can effective leadership be defined solely in terms of competence, organizational structure and management skills. Rather it must include a commitment to the demonstration of sound character by all members of the learning community, creating an environment built on virtues like mutual respect and responsibility.

Mary Aranha, utilizing her classroom as well as administrative experience, presents a compelling argument for the role of leadership in character development.

For further information about this video, see page 103.

# Foreword

*With public sentiment, nothing can fail; without it, nothing can succeed. Consequently, he who molds public sentiment goes deeper than he who enacts statutes or pronounces decisions.* —Abraham Lincoln

*A good leader accomplishes, but a great leader influences.*
—A student leader, Southwestern College

I first met Mary Aranha in February, 1996, at the annual conference of the Character Education Partnership in Washington, D.C. At the time, she was principal of the award-winning Benjamin Foulois Elementary School in Maryland. As we talked, it quickly became clear that she had a special passion for character education and all the things that make a school a good place to be. By the end of our conversation, I knew I wanted her to give one of the keynotes at our College's upcoming annual Summer Institute in Character Education.

She did, and for the hundred of teachers and school administrators who heard her, it was an unforgettable moment. She told the story—in a warmly personal, riveting, and richly detailed way—of the remarkable transformation of Benjamin Foulois School. She described her philosophy of leadership and her manner of working with people. On their evaluation forms, our Institute partici-pants said things such as, "What an inspiring leader and human being!", "I would love to work for her!" and "Her talk made the whole trip worthwhile."

The effect she had on people was not ephemeral. A year later, when I was doing a follow-up workshop at one of the schools that had attended our Institute, a teacher took me aside to tell me that her principal changed her whole approach to administration after hearing Mary Aranha speak. "She used to have very poor people skills," this teacher said. "She's like a different person now—so much more positive."

Mary Aranha has since served as character education coordinator for the state of Maryland and emerged as a national figure in the character education movement. She has lectured at conferences all across the country. The warmth and wisdom so many of us have appreciated in her speeches is, with the publica-tion of this splendid book, now accessible to a much wider audience. Leadership of schools—indeed, leadership in any domain—should be the better for it.

When I had the honor of being asked to write a foreword for *A Good Place To Be*, I happened to be reading another intriguing book—*Lincoln on Leadership* by Donald T. Phillips. In his preface, Phillips writes:

Having been in the business world for many years now, mostly in large corporate settings, I am still amazed that, of the hundreds of managers and supervisors I've encountered, I can count on one hand the number of real leaders among them. Many of these men and women have been corrupted by power; most tend to pressure or dictate when simple suggestions or recommendations would suffice. And almost always there is a lack of understanding of the simple points of human nature, such as a person's reaction at being ordered to do something rather than being asked his or her opinion.

For lessons on leadership, Phillips argues, we can't do better than look to Lincoln. He is viewed as the greatest leader this nation has ever known or will ever know, and 125 years after his death still inspires and moves people from all around the globe. The chapter titles of Phillips's book convey the secrets of Lincoln's success as a leader. For example: Get Out of the Office and Circulate Among the Troops; Build Strong Alliances; Persuade Rather Than Coerce; Honesty and Integrity Are the Best Policies; Never Act Out of Vengeance or Spite; Have the Courage to Handle Unjust Criticism; Exercise a Strong Hand—Be Decisive; Lead by Being Led; Set Goals and Be Results-Oriented; Encourage Innovation; *Preach a Vision and Continually Reaffirm It.*

As I considered these lessons from Lincoln and Mary Aranha's book, I couldn't help being struck by the parallels. If good leadership is good leadership in any sphere of life—be it the principal's office or the Oval Office—it's probably because people are people wherever you find them. Lincoln cared about people and understood human nature. He knew that people respond best when they are treated with respect, consulted, challenged, and affirmed. He knew that leaders need *willing* followers.

The same deep respect for and insight into people fill the pages of the book you are about to read. It is an uplifting and instructive story—one I commend to anyone, in any walk of life, who wants to be an effective leader.

TOM LICKONA
AUTHOR, *EDUCATING FOR CHARACTER*
DIRECTOR, CENTER FOR THE 4TH AND 5TH RS (RESPECT AND RESPONSIBILITY)
STATE UNIVERSITY OF NEW YORK AT CORTLAND

# Acknowledgments

To all the Benjamin Foulois Traditional Academy Community—the entire staff, students and the community during the period 1988-1996. You all are what made our school "A Good Place To Be!" You will always occupy a special place in my heart.

Thanks to Alex Balla, the principal in Monroeville, Pennsylvania, who encouraged me to be an administrator. A special thanks to Dr. John A. Murphy who, in 1988 as the superintendent of the Prince George's County Public Schools, appointed me principal and had the confidence in me to be a successful leader. Many thanks to Dr. Thomas Lickona, a man of high standards who encouraged me to write this book. Thoughtful memories of Dr. Jesse L. Freeman, Area V assistant superintendent in 1988 are extended.

A warm thanks to Stephanie Tayman, a friend, colleague, and supporter who constantly provides positive feedback to me. Thank you to Don Bohl, my editor, who could feel and internalize my passion as he edited this project. And to Robert and Helene Hanson, National Professional Resources Incorporated, my publishers, special thanks.

Finally, a generous thank you to all of the many individuals who've inspired and motivated me to continue my passion for ethical leadership and to create caring communities for adults and children. I believe that these communities maximize the potential of each person involved.

# Contents

# 1

## The Story

*Sometimes, life is what happens when you're making other plans.*
                                                    –Source unknown

"Take your coat off, Mary, and go over to the head office right now," Jesse said.

Dr. Jesse Freeman was one of the area assistant superintendents of Maryland's Prince George's County school district. I had been standing in his office, adjacent to the Benjamin Foulois Elementary School, for about ten minutes. That was long enough to hear what he had to say and to make one phone call—but not long enough to really take in what had just happened.

It was Monday, November 14, 1988, 9:49 a.m., and I had just been appointed principal of one of the largest elementary schools in Maryland's Prince George's County.

It was a strange feeling. On occasion, I had thought that, yes, perhaps some day I might become a principal. As an area specialist in charge of staff development and support, I saw it as a logical next step. I also believed that if some day I *were* offered a principalship, I would certainly have time to think and plan before starting the job.

Yet, here I was. I was about to walk into a very troubled school, in the middle of a school term, as a newly appointed principal, with a scandal about to break, with newspaper and maybe even television reporters waiting to badger me with questions, *and I didn't even have time to take off my coat.*

That's how the story of my eight years with the Benjamin Foulois Elementary School begins. The story is, I think, worth telling. It's only partly my story. It's also the story of what can happen when a group of people respect each other

1

and their professions, and pool their talents for the well being of all the children in their care. It's a story about what can happen when people trust one another, and when each person looks at each other person and says, *I want to help you be all that you can be.* And it's a story that says something about the power of magnet schools to break down barriers of race and poverty and reach out, in love and joy, to children of all backgrounds.

I think, also, that it's a story about learning how to lead and nurture others, and the lessons apply not just in schools, but in all aspects of life. I hope that parents will read this book, too, and be inspired to use the ideas with their children. I hope that community leaders and those who work with children in any capacity—as coaches, Scout leaders, leaders of faith-based youth groups—will see that "they can do it too," that they can lead in ways that empower young people to believe in themselves, to be all they can be.

## One Crisp November Morning…

Let me get back to the story. The day had started routinely enough. That particular morning, I had been assigned to visit a middle school and monitor the administering of the California Achievement Test (CAT), the standardized test given at that time in the school system. This was one of my tasks as an area specialist. I absolutely loved my job and felt a close collaboration with the principals and total staff of my assigned schools. When I walked into the middle school early that November morning, the principal met me at the door. "Mary, I received a call and you're to report back to the area office right away. I don't know why."

I remember feeling anxious, wondering what the problem could be. I was married with three children attending middle and high schools, and I drove back hoping not to hear any bad news about any of them.

Then, it crossed my mind that it might have something to do with the news we had heard the previous Friday.

Jesse held staff meetings with all the area specialists on Fridays. Last Friday, as usual, we met in the area conference facility, part of the same complex as the Benjamin Foulois school. During one of the breaks, a secretary, Ina, pulled me aside with the words, "Mary, come here, girl. I've got something to tell you." I said to myself, *what is it?* And she said, "Oh, everything's just broken loose."

She whispered a story about something that had happened at a staff party back in October. A reporter for the *Washington Post* had learned about the event and was here, asking all sorts of questions. I hadn't been in the school that day back in October and didn't know anything about it, so I pulled Jesse aside and told him what I had just learned. Jesse said he would take care of it, and he did.

Yes, that October event was something the newspapers could make into a scandal, if they had a mind to. But no story had appeared in the papers, so I hadn't thought any more about it.

When I arrived, Jesse walked up to me and got right to the point. The principal of the Benjamin Foulois school had been removed from office. "Mary, the superintendent has appointed you to be the principal of this school," Jesse said. "He called me this morning and said, I want Mary to be the principal." Jesse paused, then added. "Please understand.... I didn't have anything to do with it."

I understood what he meant with that last statement. He knew how much I enjoyed my role as area specialist, and he knew that the tasks ahead of me would not be easy.

"I need to call my husband," I said. My family responsibilities—especially attending to my children—were of utmost importance. When Fred answered, I wasted no words. "I've just been appointed to be principal of a school. What do you think?"

"I'll support you." That's all he needed to say. I knew what he meant: whatever needed to be done to help with the children, cooking, housework— whatever support would be needed to assist me in being a success in this new endeavor and still be a successful parent and spouse—he would be there for me.

I put down the phone and turned to Jesse. "When do I start?" That's when he spoke the words, "Take off your coat and get over to the office right away." Then he added, "That reporter is here again. There may be more. They'll want to talk to you."

The scandal—if we can call it that—involved something that had happened on a teacher-in-service day. No children were involved, just the principal and secretarial staff. Clearly, the superintendent and others saw the event as inappropriate, and the principal had been removed. If anything else was involved, I didn't know about it and didn't want to know. My job wasn't to make judgments; my role was to focus on the future and help these teachers and students create the best possible place to learn and grow.

Unfortunately, the press was there to see if they could make the principal's removal into something newsworthy—some kind of exposé. Magnet schools, you see, attract media attention as well as students. The district was under a desegregation court order, and this meant that a lot of people were watching to see how the Benjamin Foulois school would perform. The fact that this was a racially integrated school (79 percent African-American) set in the middle of a white neighborhood gave it even more visibility. And the fact that the school was not living up to its potential, based on standard test scores, didn't help. Here was a chance for the press to show, once again, how the schools were failing.

As I walked toward my new office, I passed a conference room and saw one of the secretaries sitting there, crying. Her husband stood beside her, offering comfort. A reporter was standing in a vestibule interviewing staff members. She made a beeline for me and demanded a statement.

I responded without thinking. "The staff and I are going to make sure that this is one of the best elementary schools for learning in Maryland."

That's all I was going to say. I don't get any joy out of thinking about adversity that has happened to people. This wasn't anything joyful to celebrate, and dwelling on the event would make absolutely no positive contribution.

In the days that followed, I refused to watch any news on television, or read any newspaper stories about the event.

Alone in my new office that first day, I realized I knew nothing about the people who made up the school, nothing about the school's culture. I only knew one thing. *I cared about people, loved children.*

Once the shock wore off, I went to the head secretary and told her to announce that there would be a meeting for all staff members, including support staff, at the end of the day. I had no idea what I was going to say to them; all I knew was that I had to talk to them.

I had all sorts of emotions as I sat there. Feelings of excitement, uncertainty, happiness, and anxiety faded in and out, and mixed with those feelings was a sense of strength—*that I could help make something good happen.* I couldn't wait to meet them.

The school was at a standstill that day. Anxiety, even fear, showed on the faces of staff I met in the hallways. Sounds from the classrooms were muffled—none of the happy chatter that comes when children experience the joy of learning. Even the children wore somber expressions, their eyes downcast. Something had gone very wrong with this school.

## A Chance to Talk…Really Talk to These People

Finally, it was meeting time. When I walked into the large library at about 3:45 p.m., you could hear a pin drop. All eyes were on me, waiting for me to speak, and I watched them in return. My first observation was on the racial composition of the staff—80 to 90 percent white. *There isn't much diversity here,* I thought.

My presentation was totally spontaneous and unplanned. The only thing I knew in advance was that I was *not* going to mention the scandal. I began to greet them and tell them that I was looking forward to working with them, and that together we could make the school the best elementary school in the district—no, *the best in Maryland.*

I don't remember exactly what I said, but I do remember feeling this surge of strength come over me—*this was my opportunity to really talk to this staff.* I said I was very knowledgeable about instruction, that I really cared about education, and that I was a very serious and business-like person about my work. And I said I had a lot of respect for the profession.

I went on and on like that, and I felt this strength, like someone or something was pushing. How do you explain the feeling? It was like a force was coming out of me. I was standing there, talking, telling them who I was and what I believed, and there was this energy—not my own—shaping my words and giving them power. They were listening, really listening, taking in every word.

I told them that children are important and that we would create a caring, learning environment that would be the best for every child to learn in.

I told them that I cared about all of them and that each of them was special, but that no one was any more special than anyone else.

I said that I knew a lot about education and had talents, but that I didn't know everything. I said that I respected them as adults and professionals, and I told them that they knew some things that I didn't. I told them that by putting our talents together, we could create a great school.

This was a *big* school, I said. I emphasized that—that this was a *big* school, and that I couldn't do everything myself. They would need to help, they would need to put their talents to work, and that we would do it together.

I wish I could remember more of what I said. I can't. What I remember so clearly is the feeling of that special strength flowing through me and shaping my words.

When I went back to my office, some of the staff were sitting there, waiting for me. Now, I didn't really know these people. I had seen then in the halls as I went back and forth in the building, because my office as an area specialist had been there, but I didn't know them. I remember one fellow. He ended up being the wing coordinator, the person who worked with special needs students. He was in charge of getting them placed and making sure they had the right teaching and training according to their "individual education plans," they call them "IEPs." He had asked me for some resource material in the past, and I had given it to him. Other than that, I didn't know him, and he didn't know me.

He came to me and said, "I always wanted to work with someone who was businesslike and professional. I will be your right hand. I will help you do whatever you need to do to make this work."

Others wanted to talk with me. They spoke their concerns—so many discipline problems, so many suspensions, cliques among staff members, low test scores, no core of shared values, no common commitment, no traditions, no organizational culture. They let me know that an atmosphere of low staff morale and discouragement had been hanging over this school for a long time.

Others let me know that they weren't too happy about what had happened that day. They felt that a change of administration would only make matters worse. A few made no secret about it: *They wanted their former principal back!*

---

### First Impressions

She walked into the building, statuesque, class personified, dignity exuding from her smile, her carriage. We had fun at our school— Well, what I really mean is we did pretty much what we wanted. Now, I said to myself, exactly how did *she* think *she* could make it better?

She called a staff meeting and introduced herself. After giving us her educational background, she began talking about a "vision," the way she knew our school could be. She talked about family, how the students were our children.

Well, I knew I didn't have to worry about any of that stuff! *I was only a secretary*—hired to do the menial and tiresome tasks that made it easier for teachers and administrators to run the school.

She asked each of us to introduce ourselves and tell what we could bring to this "family" she was talking about. What could I bring? I had newly self-taught typing skills, and a GED I had earned only months prior. I had nothing to give—well, nothing but love for the children.

At least, that's what I thought. Oh, my! Did I have something to learn!

— Debbie Balint, Secretary

---

## Seeing Ourselves as Others See Us

I do a lot of self-reflection, and I like to believe that I understand myself and see myself clearly. I've often wondered, however, how others—especially staff members—saw me, not just that first day, but during all my years at the school. When I started to write this book, I decided to get back in contact with some of the staff. I asked them to give me their reflections of me and of the things we did, to tell how they saw me and the programs we implemented together.

Understandably, many of the responses focused on the positive things we did. That's good. It's true that people learn from their mistakes, but perhaps they learn even more by looking at their successes—by understanding how they set forces in motion that led to a better life for everyone.

Here and elsewhere in the book, you'll find excerpts from their reflections. Their comments have greatly helped me understand what we did right, as well as where our plans came up short of our mutual goals. The box on the facing page and the box, below, give some idea of how staff members felt during that first meeting.

---

## Changing Expectations

Before the change in leadership, Benjamin Foulois was a school where you followed the respective teacher's manual and didn't ask a lot of questions. (Those who did were treated as inferior.) There was a secret policy to keep classroom doors closed and deal with your own discipline problems. The front office didn't need any more PS-74 forms than it already had. The school had so many suspensions it was embarrassing—mostly in-school suspensions. Heaven forbid parents should be inconvenienced for their children's poor behavior! Obviously, the administration did not have high expectations for students, teachers or parents.

I did a lot of praying that year before Mrs. Aranha arrived, but I was not responsible for what happened next. The principal was removed! Immediately, this strong, very professional, very determined woman walked in Monday morning. It was obvious she had done a lot of homework on the school dynamics. She came ready to clean house.

We had a staff meeting, and it was clear that we would be following a different agenda—attitudes, academics, behaviors (students and staff), cleanliness of the building, teacher dress and promptness—the list of expectation went on and on…. Poor habits would not be accepted.

One other thing was very clear. This new principal was a meticulous role model. If she expected a behavior, you can guarantee she was already following through with it herself.

—Janet Orben McMillan

---

## Why Me?

Let me get back to the story. Jesse had told me that I was to talk with Dr. John A. Murphy, the superintendent, at his office at the end of the day. I arrived there at about 5:00 p.m.

"I thought about this the whole weekend," Dr. Murphy said. "I decided that you were the person who could do what needed to be done."

He spoke in a calm, confident voice as he described the problems at the school—the same problems I had heard from the staff. Then he added one more, "There's a group of parents that can only be described as clandestine." I had no idea what he meant.

"I want you to make all those problems die," he said. "I know how much you like staff development. Here is your chance to do your staff development and see the fruits of your work. If I can ever do anything to help, let me know. Good luck."

As I drove home, I became very curious about something. *He chose me—someone who had no experience as principal—to fix the problems at a troubled school. But how did he know anything about me?"*

True, we knew each other by name and position, and we had said "hello, how are you" to each other at dozens of meetings. Yes, I had worked hard and tried to do my best in everything, giving respect to people and respect to my profession. But what had I done to merit his attention? We had never sat down for anything like a professional interview; nor had we ever had any meaningful, one-on-one dialogue about educational issues. What had I ever done that would make me stand out in his eyes?

Then I put the pieces together. At the end of each school year, the superintendent met with each area superintendent and his or her area specialists. Each of us gave an analysis of the school's instructional program, culture, and leadership. Also, he had heard me give comments at meetings. *Perhaps I was observed and interviewed for the job when I didn't even know it.*

Dr. Murphy was a fireball of a man. At the start of the school year, he had called everyone together—custodians, secretaries, teachers, everyone—for a meeting at the Capital Center, a stadium where professional sports were played. He told us he had high expectations for all of us, and after the speech, we felt motivated to do the best we could for the children. He was the kind of man who let people fly—let them soar—on their own talents, without much supervision. He provided you with ongoing staff development training and resources. He also communicated with you. If you called him, he personally returned that call by the end of the day. He was also visible—not the kind of person who kept his office door closed and never walked around to see how people were doing.

I felt his confidence and trust in me take hold. That trust was a precious gift, a validation of who I was and what I believed in. He was going to allow me to be the best that I could be—and I was going to do the same for every person on my staff. Jesse would be there to help, whenever I needed him. I remember telling him thanks for his support. And Jesse said, "Mary, you're a natural leader!"

"Thank you," I said. "You know, I would never have known it if you hadn't told me." That's so true. Sometimes we really don't know our own talents. We need others to help us see ourselves better and find our talents—and others need us to do the same for them.

Also, Fred's love and support would keep me from falling. There were people on the staff, like that special education coordinator, who had always wanted to work with someone who was truly professional. I would give them that chance.

Together, we would fly, we would soar, we would build a school in which everyone cared about each other and cared deeply about children!

## Building "A Good Place To Be"

So what happened in the school? We saw small changes the first year, and larger changes in three years. The stack of discipline referrals—as many as twenty per day—got smaller and smaller, to the point we had to deal with perhaps one referral each month. The number of suspensions—as high as thirty one year—dropped to one or zero per year. The test scores increased incrementally each year. The attendance figures climbed for both students and staff. The support staff began to assume leadership roles and continue in those roles to this day. Five of the six elementary instructional assistants who aspired to be principals are now successful principals, with one of them heading a Blue Ribbon School.

Parents began taking their children out of private and parochial schools and putting them in our school. Our students became our best ambassadors for the new culture. When a new child arrived, they would tell the newcomer what was expected: "In this school, people care about each other. We don't fight or call names or hurt feelings."

Teachers worked collegially. We became a community of leaders and a community of learners. We nurtured a sense of professionalism among all staff members, maintenance workers and secretaries as well as teachers. We had a common language. The day-to-day operation of the school was guided by a set of values and standards that we created together. We shared a common vision. We were values led, people centered, achievement oriented, and we accepted the challenges, pressures, and obstacles together as a community. We had no labor-management relations problems or employee problems. We had an excellent curriculum that met the needs of a diverse population. We celebrated with rituals and ceremonies. We improved our school from within.

In 1996, when I left the school, I walked through the halls with the realization that I had become the coach for a truly dedicated staff. I was the head leader and learner, coaching a community of leaders and learners.

Our school motto, "A Good Place to Be," had become a reality. Children liked coming to school because they not only learned but were also treated with respect and care. Educators liked working in our school because they could use their talents to improve our school, and they were treated with respect and care.

Parent involvement increased. Parents knew that staff cared about their children's academic learning and also their total well being as people.

The school received several awards. It was nominated for the Blue Ribbon School award, and I was nominated (by the staff) for the Washington Post Leadership Award. The school received awards from the Board of Education and the Maryland Center for Character Education for its Ethical Citizenship Program.

In 1994, the Council of Governments, an organization representing all of the governments within the Washington, DC, metropolitan area, selected the school's Ethical Citizenship Program as one of six best practices for building character and preventing violence. The Council exists to address issues of mutual concern, with an emphasis on developing regional approaches to common problems. It recommended that the Ethical Citizenship Program be implemented in all schools in the area.

The Ethical Citizenship Program played a very special and important role in helping us change the culture at the Benjamin Foulois Academy. Chapter 10 provides more information on that program.

The school underwent a cultural transformation, and that transformation led to success. Did I do it as principal? No! *We* did it as a total staff! Staff members enjoyed the freedom to be the professional educators they had always wanted to be, and they made the change happen.

The trust and confidence that had been placed in me was empowering. It enabled me to use my talents in special ways. I was able to pass that same sense of empowerment on to the staff.

The following chapters sketch in some of the things we did to accomplish our goals. Each chapter will end by looking at some of the insights into leadership we discovered as we worked together. These insights are ways leaders can look into themselves to reach their full potential, and ways they can interact with others to help those people achieve their full potential. I truly believe that the staff and I learned something very valuable at the Benjamin Foulois school—and that others can learn from our experience.

## Leadership Insights

Regardless of your leadership position—as boss, parent, teacher, or as leader of a volunteer organization—you are going to have to deal with unexpected events. You may not always have the time to think through a detailed action plan, or you may not even have the chance to plan what you are going to say.

When this happens, you need to rely on your basic values—on what you know in your deepest heart to be fair, right, responsible, and compassionate. Those values *are one source of power—and that power will shape your words and actions.* Your words will touch something powerful in your listeners—you will be able to *feel* them listening. In their deepest hearts, they too know what is fair, right, responsible, and compassionate. And they want to act on those values.

A second source of strength comes from recognizing how other people have validated you and placed their confidence in you. Your colleagues, family members, friends, supervisors respect you. They believe in you and will be at your side to help you. *By showing respect for and confidence in the people around you, and showing that you are there to help them, you provide them with this second source of strength.*

These two ideas—values-based actions and respect for and confidence in others—are the beginning of what we call empowerment. When people are empowered, they have the strength to put the negative feelings aside, to step away from the failures or embarrassments of the past, and to focus on a positive future.

# 2

## The School

*I deeply cared about those 36, hormonally unbalanced, street-slick students in my classroom. But what was frightening to me as an educator was that, for many students, academics had become secondary. Many children didn't come to school ready to learn—lack of sleep, empty stomachs, poor attitudes—how could they be ready?*

—Janet Orben McMillan, from her reflections about
teaching at the Benjamin Foulois Academy.

What was this place that I walked into one crisp November morning?

The Benjamin Foulois Traditional Academy is nestled in a wooded area in the town of Morningside, Maryland—a beautiful two-story building in a "country club" setting. It has a full gym, large multipurpose room, full library, and large cafeteria. The building had originally served as a junior high school and had been converted to a magnet school and named  Benjamin Foulois Traditional Academy one year before my arrival.

Morningside was a predominately white, working-class community of about 1,200 citizens, located only a few miles from the District of Columbia. It was a community of modest, well-kept homes, the kind of community where people took walks in the evening and everyone knew his neighbor. In 1987, Morningside found itself hosting a magnet school where 79 percent of the students were African-American. White students accounted for only 16 percent. Three percent were Asian, 1 percent Hispanic, and 1 percent Native American.

Magnet schools were one component of the district's System of Choice design, introduced in 1985 as a response to the need to bring the schools within court-ordered racial guidelines. The Academy's student population was drawn from a large geographic area, and the school served students from urban, suburban, and small-town neighborhoods. While some of the students shot baskets in the driveways of their suburban homes or played in the neighborhood parks, others played inside to avoid the violence outside the door, violence that has come to be associated with urban poverty. Many of our students knew the effects of poverty all too well. Thirty-seven percent of the students qualified for free or reduced-cost lunches.

## The Mothers' Patrol

My first weeks there were the roughest time in my professional life. Some of the things—like the "clandestine group of parents" Dr. Murphy had warned me about—I can laugh about now.

You could see them in the school every day, this group of concerned mothers. If I looked out my window, I might see one or more on the playground. If I walked through the cafeteria, a mother would be there. They even patrolled the bathrooms. And at the end of the day, when school was dismissed, they gathered to make sure everything was in order. They were on patrol, looking for "ways to make the school better," and—believe me—they saw it as their high moral duty to provide me with advice.

I learned to set aside time each day to hear the reports. A child had heard some bad language on the playground. *How was I going to handle that?* the parent would demand. A child had reported to her parent that a classmate had hit another child, and that *the teacher hadn't done anything about it. What was I going to do about it?*

"I'm an architect," one mother told me and asked me to step into the cafeteria. "See, there's a crack in your ceiling. Somebody is going to get hurt when it falls."

I knew she wasn't an architect; she was a housewife. I went looking for the crack—looking real hard, squinting at the ceiling from every possible angle. I couldn't find any crack, and neither could my head custodian.

They demanded a meeting with Jesse and me at night to discuss problems in the school, and they asked to tape record the meeting. I declined the invitation.

They asked permission to photocopy papers to be sent home with all the children, to get a petition going to reinstate their principal. "It's not because of anything you've done," the leader of the patrol said.

"Well, I'm not going to use the school copy machine to run off literature like that," I said. "You'll have to go somewhere else."

One mother in particular averaged four trips a day, wearing a different outfit each time. Was this some kind of fashion show? Any excuse to get into the school and even into the classroom would do. Once, she brought three coats for her first grader so that he would have a choice of what coat to wear when he came home.

Every little thing—events on the playground or the lunchroom, the cleanliness of the bathrooms, the way a teacher had talked to a student, a discipline problem in the hallway—everything was reported to me in detail, so that I could take the proper action.

You see, this group of mothers had attended this school when it was a junior high school, graduated from high school, married, and returned to the neighborhood, living next door or down the street from their parents. Now their children were attending the school, which was now much different. Most of them had never interacted with diverse cultures.

I knew what they were doing. They were trying to do everything in their power to make me snap. They didn't know that the more they did, the stronger I got. I can remember standing at my desk. I would stand up there, with a little voice inside me saying, *Stay in control. They are trying to get you to say some- thing or to do something so that they can report it to the school board or to the superintendent. Don't flip. They are trying to get you angry. Control your emotions.* So, I would stand up sometimes, and I would have my fingernails dug into the bottom of my desk. I wanted to say, *How dare you say that there are discipline problems here that I'm not handling. I've been here three weeks!*

I learned to use my nicest, calmest voice. "Well, thank you for reporting that. I'll be sure to handle that; I'll be sure to look into it. And I will be sure to get back to you."

The mothers' patrol had been around before I came on board. The former principal was white, and these mothers were white. Maybe they felt they needed to keep in close contact with the principal, as a way of watching out for their children. The principal had catered to their wishes. Now, all of a sudden, they see this tall, strong African-America woman come along, and she has different expectations and a different leadership style.

I couldn't compromise my beliefs. I believe in diversity, and I believe in respecting everybody. I believe in inclusion, in putting special needs students into regular classrooms whenever possible, so that students from each group learn to respect each other. I don't believe in cliques. I believe in being fair to everyone.

I stood firm in my beliefs and my desire to do what was best for children. You see, I was a mother, parent, teacher, and administrator, and I knew that human beings had needs, and that they made errors, but that those errors should be an educational process for them. I also knew that if you led your life and did your work based on a sound set of values, you couldn't help but succeed.

## Finding Perspective and Guidance

If you haven't already guessed it, I love proverbs, aphorisms, and wise sayings of any kind, as well as inspirational poems and stories. I've been collecting these throughout my professional career, and I use them for both my own and my staff's motivation and sense of direction during difficult times. You'll find many of my favorite sayings and inspirational poems interspersed throughout this book.

The little poem titled "Anyway" gives some perspective to the mothers' patrol and other situations where we are challenged to deal with people who have a view different from our own.

### Anyway

People can be unreasonable, illogical and self-centered.
> Love them anyway.
If you do good, people may accuse you of selfish, ulterior motives.
> Do good anyway.
If you are successful, you may win false friends and true enemies.
> Succeed anyway.
The good you do today may be forgotten tomorrow.
> Do good anyway.
Honesty and frankness may make you vulnerable.
> Be frank and honest anyway.
People follow only top dogs, but favor underdogs.
> Be sympathetically wise anyway.
What you spend days building may be destroyed overnight.
> Build anyway.
People really need help, but may be critical if you help them.
> Help them anyway.
Give your profession the best that you have and you'll be remembered....
> Anyway.

—Author unknown

## Magnetic Power—Responding to Diversity

If anything, dealing with the mothers helped me confirm how important magnet schools can be. You see, Benjamin Foulois was not only a magnet school; it was also a "Traditional Academy." The school featured a highly structured curriculum. Students wore uniforms. Latin was offered in the sixth grade.

The program was available to all students with no entry exam. Parents' interest in sending their children to a traditional academy and the school's compliance with desegregation guidelines were the only criteria for admission.

Diversity applied to special-needs students as well. The school served as one of only nine special education schools in the county that provided Intensity V services. These are services for students with documented disabilities that require a comprehensive setting with related services for all or most of the school day. Intensity V students made up more than 10 percent of the total school population.

At the time of my leadership, the school consisted of thirty-one self-contained classrooms from kindergarten to sixth grade, and nine special education classes. The average class size for regular education students was thirty. For special education, class size was nine.

The school ran with a total staff of seventy-two, including special resource teachers, subject area specialists, paraprofessionals, librarians, a part-time counselor, clerical personnel, custodians, and food service workers. The teaching staff consisted of twenty-two regular education teachers and nine special education teachers.

Enrollment in 1988 was approximately 750 students, and this increased to over 800 in the following years. We needed to find ways of serving all these students, of helping each and every one develop to their full potential.

## Establishing a New Agenda

By the end of the school year, I knew the movers and shakers and the people who influenced others. They also got to know me. I was a new and different personality, someone with a leadership style very different from my predecessor. I had high expectations for staff students, parents, and myself. I believed in excellence in performance and in accountability. People knew I cared, that I was enthusiastic and energetic, and that I expected the best from myself and everyone else.

My most important task that first year was making sure that morale was up so that students would have motivated teachers. High morale and motivation are so important, so essential for effective education.

Much of my energy that first year was used to put strategies in place for building trusting relationships between administration and staff, staff and students, and staff and parents. Staff members had opportunity to dialogue with me, and teams had opportunity to work together to become true teams. Staff was included in planning and had input into decision making, using the school-based management process. Staff members were recognized for their talents and accomplishments and provided feedback relating to their strengths and weaknesses. We developed a shared vision for the school, along with standards of personal and professional excellence.

Some of the staff did not feel they could work well in the new environment we were creating. After all, this way of doing things was very different from the former principal's, and these staff members felt they would be better off somewhere else. After the close of the school year, the school hired seventeen non-tenured teachers from across the nation. Some had never worked in our kind of school. We tried to hire the best, but also worked toward building a diverse staff that could serve a diverse student body.

Our magnet school had united African-Americans, Asians, Hispanics, and European Caucasians, along with a few Native Americans, into a learning community. This was the kind of diversity that students would be dealing with, in the real world, for the rest of their lives. The goal was to build a staff that could teach members of all ethnic groups to appreciate and respect members of the other groups.

## An Apple Cider Toast to Success

At the end of school year, the staff surprised me with a closing luncheon. I walked into the Andrews Air Force Base Officers' Club, where the luncheon was held, expecting to see only a few of my colleagues. The whole staff was there, and my husband, Fred, was standing at the head of the table, waiting to seat me. At our places were two plastic champagne glasses filled with apple cider.

Who would ever believe those two plastic glasses and a little apple cider could be so meaningful!

The social committee leader thanked me, on behalf of the staff, for my positive leadership role and for believing in them. I was so grateful for the support of these educators that I began to become emotional. It had been such a strain that first year, dealing with the remnants of the activities left from the previous administration.

Little did I know that what had started out to be such a challenge would become the reason why I speak to leaders and staffs across the nation. I was beginning to learn what can be accomplished by developing people to their full potential. By helping people in this way, a leader achieves self-actualization of his or her own potential. Those lessons continued for the next seven years and have become the major theme of my presentations to my fellow educators.

## Leadership Insights

High morale and motivation are so important to any group, whether it's a school, a family, or a community organization. Where does this thing we call "motivation" come from?

Every once in a while, we see a book or an article in a professional publication about "how managers can motivate employees." I think that's pretty silly. Motivation comes from *within.* No one person can *motivate* another person, unless we mean the worst kind of motivation, the kind that threatens punishment if certain actions aren't taken. True, fear can be a strong motivator, but it's a motivator that comes wrapped in unhealthy tension and ultimately destroys morale.

A far healthier—and much stronger—motivation happens when a person anticipates genuine joy and satisfaction from performing a task. Leaders don't *motivate* people to have this kind of experience—how could they? Rather, they create an environment in which it happens automatically. They do so by building trusting relationships, giving people opportunity to dialogue and to participate in the planning processes, and encouraging them to use their talents and make a contribution to a worthwhile cause—and then recognizing them for their accomplishments.

# 3
# Empowerment 101

*We must be the change we want to see in the world.*
—Ghandi

*When the best leader's work is done, the people say, "We did it ourselves."*
—Lao-Tsu

*Critical to leadership is a foundation of shared values, which support great achievement. The influence on values is where the leader can most impact the organization.*
—William T. Solomon

We had a full agenda that summer as we planned for the opening of school. Many staff members had agreed to work during the summer to develop our own teachers' handbook. In addition, the staff and I had about three days together before the students returned. We took advantage of this time to set an initial climate or tone for the school year.

First, I made sure I was visible throughout the day, personally greeting each staff member. "It's great to have you back!" "You're an asset to the staff!" "How's your family?" "Is your mother better?"

These were my greetings, offered sincerely along with handshakes, pats on the shoulder, and an occasional hug. Before the three days had passed, each and every member of the staff—teachers, cafeteria workers, support staff—had received a personal acknowledgment.

You see, performance standards, test scores, academic excellence and technological skills were all very important. But if teachers are to create an environment in which students achieve these goals, some basic human needs had to be met. All of us share these common needs, an idea that Abraham Maslow emphasized in his hierarchy of human needs. After the basic needs for food and shelter are met, there is the need for safety, for love, for "connectedness" or sense of belonging, for self-esteem—and finally the need for self-actualization.

Before adults can guide, nurture or instruct young people, their needs have to be met. Now, whether this happens at home, at school, on the job, or in the community doesn't matter all that much—but the needs have to be met.

## Learning To Share Our Talents

Our initial meeting began at 9:00 A.M. the first day back for teachers. This was the beginning of many training meetings, but it was a very, very special meeting because all members of the instructional and non-instructional staff attended, including the secretaries, maintenance personnel, cafeteria workers and some members of our parent teachers association.

I had done a great deal of self-awareness reflection and now it was time for the staff to do the same. We needed to find out who we were and what kind of school culture we wanted. This was the beginning of our school transformation.

As new staff members were introduced, each was asked to describe what skill or talent he or she brought to our school. It was exciting to hear such statements as, "I'm a good listener," "I'm a very creative person," or "I'm a good writer." Then I told them what I felt I could bring to them, telling them that I saw myself as having strong instructional leadership skills and the ability to create conditions in which they would be motivated and inspired to achieve their potential.

Next, staff members were invited to share their talent/skill with another person. People aren't asked to do this very often. Initially, they all just sort of looked at each other. Then they began to talk to one another about their special abilities. Someone recorded the talents as they shared.

This was a great activity because many people shared the same talents. We heard comments like "I'm a great organizer," "I'm a good problem solver," "I love to cook," "I'm a mezzo soprano," "I'm a jazz musician," "I'm an artist," "I have computer skills" and "I get along well with people." Several people said, "My talent is patience. I can slow down and be patient when I have to."

It was phenomenal! We were building relationships with one another. And we would find ways to use the talents and special abilities of everyone in that room as we journeyed toward school improvement.

## Character-Based Standards

If the students in our care were to become self-disciplined young people who achieved socially and academically, then we needed to look for some humanistic character traits that would empower all of us—staff as well as students—to achieve these goals. We needed to be guided by character traits such as respect, caring, responsibility, fairness, empathy, honesty and courage—especially courage.

We discussed how important respect was for everyone. We said we needed to first respect ourselves as human beings, but also respect ourselves as professionals. There was a mutual understanding that our job was challenging and difficult at times, but there was a real and special reward in our profession as teachers. We would get that reward only when we truly respected our profession.

We talked about the respect we had for specific teachers when we were children, and the effect that those teachers had on our lives. You know, these adults could reflect so clearly back to the one teacher who had made the most positive impact on them. They could put themselves back in time, to when they were six or seven or ten years old, recalling tiny details of situations that took place back then. And, oh yes—they could also recall the one teacher that had left them with the most *negative* impressions.

Then I asked, "When your students become adults, which one of these teachers will you be in their memory—the one who left a positive impression, or the one who left the negative feelings?" This *really* made them start thinking.

We reinforced this idea at the meeting and throughout the school year by displaying sayings and inspirational literature reminding teachers of the lasting impressions they make on students. Some of that literature appears in the box below, on the following page, and elsewhere in this book.

---

### A Teacher's Realization

I have come to the frightening conclusion that I am the decisive element in the classroom.

It is my personal approach that creates the climate. It is my daily mood that makes the weather. As a teacher, I possess tremendous power to make a child's life miserable or joyous. I can be a tool of torture or an instrument of inspiration. I can humiliate or humor, hurt or heal. In all situations, it is my response that decides whether a crisis will be escalated or de-escalated, and a child humanized or dehumanized.

—Dr. Haim G. Ginott, *Teacher and Child* (Collier Books, 1995)

---

> ## Life is...
>
> a challenge—meet it
> a gift—accept it
> an adventure—dare it
> a sorrow—overcome it
> a tragedy—face it
> a duty—perform it
> a game—play it
> a mystery—unfold it
> a song—sing it
> an opportunity—take it
> a journey—complete it
> a promise—fulfill it
> a beauty—praise it
> a struggle—fight it
> a goal—achieve it
> a puzzle—solve it
> ——Source unknown

We talked about *respect* in all the relationships that make up a school: students' respect for adults, and adults' respect for students; administrators' respect for staff, and staff members' respect for administrators. We were very precise. How would we address each other in the presence of children, and when children were not present? How would we talk with parents? How would we show respect for support staff if some problem came up? And so on.

This led to a discussion of how we would handle our moods and anger so that we could make good decisions about our own conduct. We realized that sometimes rudeness or inappropriate behavior on the part of children could make adults angry. We said that angry adults sometimes yell at students, berate, or demean them. How were we going to behave so that our anger didn't get the best of our good judgment?

We talked about modeling, being an example. We needed to remember that we were *teachers*, and that the examples we set would help students learn alternative ways of handling anger or conflict. In fact, I told them if they ever got to the point where they felt they would say something inappropriate in a situation of anger with students, that they were to call me over the PA system. I would come to their room, or send another administrator to monitor the class, and they could come to my conference room to talk it over, or just privately cool down until they could react rationally.

We went on to talk about what *Responsibility, Fairness* and *Caring* meant to us. I recall saying that we didn't have to love each other, but we certainly needed to respect and be cordial to one another, because we had ten months of living together as a family. Again, we were very specific about what each of these words meant in our relationships with students, support staff, parents, and each other. As we talked, we had a person record our ideas on a flip chart.

We needed some rules and standards to follow. You see, by talking about these humanistic character traits, we were beginning to set standards together. We were agreeing on the specific behaviors we expected from each other.

## Standards of Expectation

All that talk is important, but now we needed some mechanism to make the ideas stick in our memory.

During the summer, I had read *The Power of Ethical Management* by Kenneth Blanchard and Norman Vincent Peale (William Morrow and Company, 1988), in which the authors list five "P words" that can be used to guide ethical decision making. We discussed ideas from the book, then took a personal approach and established our own meanings for each of the words. They were:

1. **Pride** – We said that we needed to be proud of ourselves as individuals. Each of us was unique, and we should be proud of that. We also needed to be proud of our school. We needed to market our school. We should not talk negatively about our colleagues or our students. Again, we needed to be proud of the profession. We needed to work together to make our school "A Good Place to Be."

2. **Purpose** – What was our purpose for being at our school? Someone with a sense of humor said, "To get a paycheck." We laughed, then talked seriously about always wanting to help children be their best. Many shared that they had always wanted to be a teacher and that they liked children. I shared with them that I had decided I wanted to be a teacher while in the fifth and sixth grade. I had Ms. Jackson as my teacher for those grades. She made a life-long impression on me. She taught and cared for her students extremely well. She was the consummate professional and so serious about her teaching and her students' learning!

3. **Patience** – We really helped each other with this one. You see, I'm usually an "instant" kind of person, someone who wants results *now*, right away. I realize that you have to have patience, but this is not one of my talents. I needed help from others. Remember when we discussed our talents, some people

had said that they had this talent of being able to slow down and be patient. If I felt myself getting impatient, it was time to talk to one of those people.

4. **Persistence** – We had set our standards to live by and we had a dedication and commitment to those ethical standards. I knew it would take three to five years before we would really see results. Patience was crucial, but so was persistence. We needed to maintain a balance between obtaining results and caring how we achieved them.

5. **Perspective** – We had many strategies for improving our school. We knew that there would be obstacles and challenges that would be faced daily. We would take the time to meet as a staff and as individual teams to reflect on where we were, to evaluate ourselves and to focus on where we wanted to go. Through this process, we were continuously reassessing how we would get to our destination. At the same time, we knew that achieving such improvement was ongoing, that we would always strive to be better.

As a result of our dialogue, we added two more "P's" to our standards:

6. **Perseverance** – Sometimes the many challenges and duties that would be required would become overwhelming, but we knew we had to persevere and stand by our commitment no matter how difficult. I emphasized that I would be the support and I expected excellence out of myself and out of them. I would work twice as hard and did not expect them to do any more than I was going to do.

7. **Positiveness** – Attitude would have a lot to do with whether we met our goals. Attitudes color how we feel about ourselves, the students, the parents, our personal lives…everything. A positive attitude lights the way for a bright and colorful future. A negative attitude would take us to those dark places in our past, places we didn't want to go back to.

## Burying the Past—Goodbye and Good Riddance!

I told staff that they were very bright and intelligent, and that they needed to believe in themselves. They needed to have hope and know that achieving excellence was within each of them. But just telling them this and talking about being positive wasn't enough. We needed some way to put this attitude change into action then and there. This meant we needed to look at ourselves again.

We performed an activity in which we simulated removing all of our negative baggage and attitudes (you know, the stuff human beings carry around in their heads). We actually put our hands to our heads and pretended to pull out all of the negatives. Then we conducted a burial, burying that baggage, laying it all to rest. The staff was told that they could go home and write the "negative stuff" in their private lives on paper and throw it away in the garbage. We knew that many things were truly personal; some needed to be left in the past because we couldn't do anything about these things anyway.

We took the position that we could not function clearly with the different negative feelings, thoughts and behavior that many of us had internalized. We decided that we would not entertain negativity. When someone was negative, we would inject something positive. We knew that many things were habit, but all of us knew our personal strengths and weaknesses. We vowed to practice so that positiveness would become the habit.

You know, the more I reflect, the more I understand that to become a really caring, confident person who can nurture, teach and lead others, *we must feel good about who we are: both physically and emotionally.* Adults as well as children need to feel this way. Society tells us that we should look a certain way...act a certain way. I knew that as I led the school community, I had to go beyond the rhetoric and exhibit what I really felt in my heart and believed in my mind as I interacted with the adults and young people.

You see, you can accomplish anything if you have the desire, the dream, vision and a clear conscious about *who you are as a person, what you believe and what really is important in life.*

Years ago, I expressed my feelings regarding a positive self-image, and how that image affects others, in a little composition I called "From Head to Toe." I still find that composition useful, and I hope you will too. It appears on the next page.

## The Power of Self-Reflection

That initial staff meeting was the foundation for our success. Our future faculty meetings and in-service times became ongoing staff development and personal development meetings. All of us became empowered and realized how each of us could make a difference in the social and academic achievement of our students, in our own professional and personal development, and in the way we involved parents in their children's education.

I don't think it would have happened if I hadn't spent countless hours thinking about who I was and what I needed to do.

During that summer before the opening of school, I had much time to reflect on the real meaning of leadership and the kind of school community I wanted to lead. I thought about all of my past educational experiences, but what I really thought about was my feelings about the importance of being an ethical leader, someone who had courage, was honest, fair, responsible and respected people regardless of their title. I wanted to bring out the best in all of the educators, students and parents that I faced during those challenging times the previous year.

## From Head to Toe

**The Head** – It doesn't matter whether the head is big or small, it should hold positive thoughts of yourself and others. Let's use the brain to think of ways we can be a better person, serve others and create ways to assist others to be their best.

**The Eyes** – It doesn't matter what color they are. The eyes can see the beauty in the earth, nature, trees, flowers and man. The eyes can see the best in people and not the worst. They can see the beautiful rainbow of colors in people, a rainbow that makes us beautifully different.

**The Ears** – No matter how big or small, we can use them to listen to the sounds of music and the voices of kind words instead of negative words.

**The Mouth** – Size and shape don't matter, but the utterance of kind words does. "I care about you." "You're special." "Thank you. "How can I help?" "How are you feeling?" "You did a great job." "It's a beautiful day." "I'll share with you." "I love you." These words should be expressed many times. But just as important, the mouth should be used to share a smile with someone.

**The Arms** – Long or short, they should be used to give a hug. Remember when you were a child, how good being hugged felt? The child grows up to be an adult, but still a human being. So give a hug to someone today.

**The Hands** – Large or small, hard or soft, your hands have their own language. A handshake says a lot. "I respect you." "How are you, I'm glad to see you." The touch of the hand or a pat on the back speaks in a time of happiness or sadness. Never use the hand to show anger. They're not intended for abuse or hurt. Rather, form a tight circle, then grasp your hands together in the center, showing that you've come together as a team."

**The Feet** – Use the feet to walk the talk, showing what you believe. Step up and be responsible for your actions. Stand tall and make good choices. Be empathetic and put your feet in the shoes of others.

**The Heart** – A healthy heart loves mankind and has feelings for others. Feel, feel, feel with the heart. Be cautious not to break the heart of others.

WHEN WE PUT THESE ATTRIBUTES TO OUR PHYSICAL FEATURES, WE CAN THINK MORE CLEARLY ABOUT OUR PURPOSE AND ACCOMPLISH OUR GOALS.

I looked at myself to discover what kind of person I really was. I was a very positive person; most of the literature I had read for leisure was related to bettering myself, handling my anger and moods constructively….so as to make good decisions. I certainly had to practice that during that previous school year. Also, I realized that I was a very caring and empathetic person who always thought how I would feel if I were in the other person's shoes.

Finally, I liked people, smiled a lot and loved children, so it was easy to get along with people and handle the different personalities that were a part of working with people. I knew this about myself, but I thought it was very important to let those whom I would be working with know exactly who I was and what my personal and professional standards of integrity were. My goal was to carry the staff through the same self-awareness process so that they could be equipped to inspire and motivate their students to learn academically, to maximize their potential and become the best they could be. As Roland Barth, a former leadership trainer, says, "A school can fulfill no higher purpose than to teach its members that *they* can make *what they believe in* happen."

As we had hoped, a transformation of the school's culture began to evolve. As I had hoped, I became a coach and the staff and students were empowered to make *what they believed in* become a reality. It happened! We became a community of leaders and learners: the staff, the students, parents and myself.

## Leadership Insights

People as well as groups need time for self-reflection, to determine who they are, what is truly important, and what they want to achieve. They need to reflect on their talents and special gifts, on the humanistic values that they wish to embrace, on the type of influence they wish to have on others.

Here are some questions I asked myself, and that I found useful. It is important that every leader, no matter what the context—community, home, or place of employment—ask questions such as these.

1. What are my personal strengths and weaknesses? Do I really understand myself, see myself clearly—and do I like what I see?

2. Am I in touch with my talents and special gifts? How will these affect my interaction with others and my leadership style?

3. Do I have a clear purpose for the task ahead?

4. Do I have a vision—a picture of what the future will be like when I achieve my purpose?

5. Do I have the courage to do what I believe needs to be done?

6. Am I willing to constantly try to better myself? To try new things, to keep learning and growing as a professional?

Once a leader can honestly answer "yes" to these questions, he or she can guide a group through a similar process of self-reflection and discovery. The questions for the group are very much the same: What special talents and gifts do we have in the group? Do we have a clear purpose in mind? Do we have a visual picture of what the world will look like when we achieve that purpose?

Think about it. When you're sitting beside someone in a group, and you learn that he or she has a talent for, say, art or music, or the gift of empathy or patience, you've learned something very meaningful about that person. You've begun to form a bond with that individual. And when you discover that every person in that group will be using his or her talents to achieve a shared vision, that bond deepens. The future becomes brighter, illuminated by that vision, and each and every person's talents give assurance that the vision can become real.

The group exercises we used during those first meetings are not new or especially innovative. Similar exercises are often used in business retreats and other kinds of meetings. Rituals are important. I know of one company retreat, for example, in which the executives wrote "all the negative stuff"—stuff about company politics, turf battles, and finger-pointing—on sheets of paper, then everyone went outside and actually burned the papers in a bonfire. Also, memory devices like the "Five P's" make ideas stick in the mind. They create a common language.

As a leader, you know what your group needs. As you do your own self-reflection, you will likely discover what kinds of group-reflection are important.

# 4

## A Community of Professionals

*Trust men and they will be true to you; treat them greatly and they will show themselves great.*                                  –Ralph Waldo Emerson

*How do you recognize a leader? His people consistently turn in superior performances.*                                    —Robert Townsend

From the first day I walked into the school, I couldn't help noticing the floors. They were like mirrors, a minor miracle when we consider that 800 plus pairs of shoes scuffed and tracked across those tiles each day. The person responsible turned out to be a man named Anthony, the building supervisor. When I met him, I told him his floors were so shiny I could use them as a mirror to put on makeup. He laughed at that. In the months that followed, I learned that Tony (as he was called) was a real professional, very proud of his work and the work of his staff.

If this empowerment idea was going to work, it would have to be for everyone—not just teachers, but for people like Tony on the maintenance staff, the secretaries, the cafeteria workers, and everyone else. We did just that—we were able to make the idea work.

To explain how this happened, I need to backtrack and tell about some of the other things we did during the summer before that first full year of school.

During the summer, I asked Tony to prepare job responsibilities for his position as well as all the members of his building maintenance staff. Not only did he develop written job responsibilities as requested, he asked to meet with me so that he could explain each job. Little did he know, as he talked, that he would be doing a presentation on the first day of school—that he would be standing in front of everyone so that he could introduce his staff and explain what they did.

When I told him, he was shocked. He had never, ever thought about presenting to anyone—especially not teachers. Yes, he spoke to everyone, but never, ever *presented* to them.

"Well," I said, "there's a first time for everything! You've done a great job explaining to me. You'll do great! " Then I added, "I'll be right beside you. I won't let you fail."

I could see his excitement building. Tony contacted his supervisor and arranged for all of the building maintenance staff (day and night personnel) to be available for a staff meeting on the morning of the first day. He let them know what we were doing and arranged to meet with me later if I wanted to go over his presentation.

Meanwhile, I had met with the head secretary, Wendy. I told her the same thing. She was to come prepared to explain the responsibilities of the Secretary I, Secretary II and our Secretary for Special Education. Wendy was nervous. "Mrs. Aranha, I never talked to all of the staff before," she said. I told her I would work with her on the presentation and would be right beside her.

The cafeteria manager met with me. She was given the same assignment and asked to get her staff to the initial meeting.

Next, I met with all of the grade level chairpersons as a group. For their presentation, they developed a schedule of the monthly meetings they would be conducting with their individual teams. They created agendas to ensure that topics like instructional strategies, strengths, weaknesses and concerns would be discussed at these meetings. The monthly meeting dates were given to me so that I could coordinate attending them.

The guidance counselor prepared a detailed description of what she would like to do to work more effectively with the administration, the staff, students and parents.

The initial meeting arrived. There was coffee, tea, and pastries, along with lots of smiles, hugs and networking. I arranged it so that the maintenance staff, secretarial staff, and cafeteria staff introduced themselves and were the first to present.

The total staff was pleasantly surprised. As I watched their faces, I could sense that they were getting the idea—they knew that we were indeed going to be an all-inclusive community. We were going to understand and respect each other, regardless of our roles.

Tony, Wendy, the cafeteria manager and the counselor all did superb jobs. The staff was most excited about Tony. We had no idea there was such a method to all of the cleaning and maintenance tasks. Someone was responsible for the vents and air-conditioning, another was responsible for this side of the building, the library. Tony was there to see that it all got done properly. All of the key support personnel were capable, professional and knew their jobs.

## We're Ready for the Students!

Everything we did during those three days set the tone for the year to start.

The day before students returned to school, the staff showed off their classrooms. Time was set aside for all staff to convene at a designated place in the building. We would begin a tour of the building, visiting each classroom. All of the teachers were very proud of their rooms as we stopped and visited them. Everyone had bright, colorful instructional bulletin boards that demonstrated lots of creativity and hard work. Colleagues would give verbal compliments or written ones. Some teachers took notes about the different ways other teachers had set up their rooms and used their class space.

After these building tours, it wasn't unusual to see some of the teachers deciding to do more in their rooms. Grade level teams gathered to share materials and ideas especially with less experienced teachers or those who were new to our school. As a closing activity on this final day of preparation, we reconvened in the meeting room. There we formed a huge circle holding hands and recited a poem entitled "Hand and Hand." It's printed on the next page.

I like this poem. Its message is simple and positive. I intended it to express the idea that we were in this together and we would be successful helping one another.

## We're People—Not Titles

That meeting opened up our ability to communicate like nothing I've ever seen before. As time went on, our job titles began to matter less and less. We were simply people who cared about the children who were to be under our care.

For example, Tony and I made it a habit to walk the building together, perusing the physical facility to make sure things were intact. This was ongoing. We took preventive measures so that our students and staff were comfortable in their physical facility. All bathrooms were made to work properly, ceiling tiles were replaced if necessary and the outside of the building was painted. We indeed had a comfortable and beautiful place to work. As we walked, we often talked about the importance of leadership and responsibility.

Then, one day I told Tony that I was granting him autonomy to do his job;

from that day on he was "Principal of Facility Maintenance," and I would work with him collaboratively to support what he needed. He rose to these expectations. Tony monitored his staff and praised them when appropriate. He also documented employees and held conferences with them when their performance didn't meet expectations. When there was no improvement, other action was taken with my support.

I met with Tony and my other leaders frequently to coach them on how to help their team members become leaders. There was no doubt about it—Tony was a professional. We shouldn't limit that term *professional* to doctors, lawyers, teachers and others with extensive college training. It should apply to anyone who is highly skilled and knowledgeable in his or her field, who sets high standards for tasks performed, and follows a code of ethics in dealing with his or her clients. Secretaries can be professionals, as can food service workers, and many others.

> ### Hand and Hand
> It's nice to be needed and
> Do you know why?
> We all must depend on the
> Other guy.
> We can work ourselves right
> Down to the bone
> But we certainly can't get the
> Job done alone.
> If everyone realized this obvious fact
> And elected right then to get into the act,
> What a wonderful place our school would be
> With me helping you
> And you helping me.
> —Author unknown

## Don't Ask A Professional To Fetch Your Ice Cubes

When I first arrived at the school, the secretaries used to go in the conference room refrigerator and get teachers ice cubes. I told them that I had taught a long time, and I had never, ever expected a school secretary to provide that sort of service for me or anyone else. I made sure they understood that they were important people, professional at their job, and that they would be treated that way.

I shared with the secretaries that they, the front office, were a reflection of me and of who we were at the school. After all, the front office was where students, visitors, parents, delivery people, and others made their initial contact with a representative of the school. We talked about greeting our parents, students and all people in a respectful manner, regardless of socioeconomics, race or behavior. We needed to make everyone who came to our school feel they were welcome. Also, this meant being professional and mindful of our own conduct, especially during those times students and parents were present in the office.

Parents were not to be ignored or made to stand waiting, even while secretaries were busy on the phone. I told them of my experience as a parent visiting a school office where I was made to wait while the secretary talked on the phone. I emphasized that it doesn't take a second to say, "I'll be with you shortly." At a minimum, they should be acknowledged and told to have a seat.

During one visit to a high school, I observed a sign on the desk of one of the office staff; it read "I'm not your mother!" What a message to relate to young people, their parents or any visitor to the school!

We also made our office atmosphere a welcoming place. The counter in the front office—you know that real, non-verbal barrier that separates and tells people stop—was removed. This opened up the work area and made it look like a professional place of business. We saw to it that the secretaries had comfortable desks and chairs. They were able to decorate their office. We collaborated on office etiquette and expectations.

I kept them informed regarding expected visitors, when special school activities (assemblies) were scheduled and anything else important to our staff, students and parents. The office staff was introduced to vendors and other individuals visiting the school. I've been in schools where the secretaries were told only what they really needed to know, and nothing more, and where they were never introduced to visitors. That's no way to treat professional colleagues!

On one occasion, the UPS deliveryman commented to me, "I love coming to this school. People really welcome you. The children seem to love working and learning." He asked, "Is this a special school?"

I told him, "Yes. It is a special place—a place for teachers to teach and children to be their best academically and socially!"

As you can see, support personnel were a key part of our school community. As a result of being knowledgeable in their job responsibilities and being trusted to perform these duties, they had become masters of their trade. They, too, felt empowered.

## Saying Goodbye to Colleagues—Necessary, but Never Easy

I don't believe in holding people back who have grown professionally. An effective leader inspires and assists employees to maximize their potential. When this is practiced, you always have good people who strive to improve. Some will put their improved skills to work in another job.

Eventually, Tony became a building supervisor at a senior high school, with a pay increase. Since that time I have called on him to present at a character education conference with over 500 participants, explaining his leadership role as building supervisor in making our school a great workplace and a great learning environment for children.

Wendy went home to care for her children. Subsequently, she opened a preschool where she implemented the core traits of respect and responsibility as guiding standards for the youngsters in her care. I have visited Wendy's preschool, which is housed in a garage her husband converted for her. It reminded me so much of the kindergarten rooms at our school. Modeling is so important and pays off for everyone.

The individuals who assumed the positions held by Tony and Wendy also became empowered. The tone of the school was one of professionalism, responsibility, and leadership, built on standards of excellence and a sense of community. Tony, Wendy, and others helped to establish that culture—and the culture lived on after they left.

## Understand this Idea of "Empowerment"

Interestingly, business executives are more familiar with the idea of empowerment than are leaders in education and nonprofit organizations. A lot was being written about empowerment during the 1990s. Many felt that American businesses had become too bureaucratic, and that traditional "command and control" management was keeping employees from being as productive and responsive to customers as they might be. The concept of empowerment is very much the same, regardless of whether we're talking about business or education. See box, "What Does Empowerment Look Like?"

Clearly, the staff grasped the idea of empowerment, as shown in former staff members' reflections on life at Benjamin Foulois. Debbie Balint, a secretary, had this to say.

> "Empowerment." I'd heard her talk about it time and again.
> Somehow I'd understood it to mean "power" or "overpowering."
> Little did I realize that this idea of empowerment was a sneaky little

## What Does Empowerment Look Like?

Warren Bennis, author of more than a dozen books on leadership in business, has devoted his entire professional life to studying what makes companies successful. In *An Invented Life* (Addison Wesley, 1993), he describes four ways to recognize whether an organization has actually achieved empowerment.

The first is that "People feel significant." They believe that the job they are doing is important and is making a difference in people's lives. Even if the task is small, routine, or menial, they see it as contributing to a larger purpose.

Second, "Learning and competence matter." Empowering leaders value learning and mastery, and the people who work for them hold the same values. Mistakes as well as successes are considered part of the learning experience.

Third, "People are part of a community." There is a feeling of teamwork, of unity, even of family.

Fourth, "Work is exciting... stimulating, challenging, fascinating, and fun." Bennis says that an empowering kind of leadership "pulls," rather than "pushes," people toward a goal. In other words, when people work under an empowering style of leadership, they are attracted to and energized by the opportunity to make a contribution to the organization's goals—employees voluntarily "enroll in an exciting vision of the future." Motivation comes through identification with that vision, rather than through anticipated rewards or punishments.

devil creeping into me without my knowledge…. Oh, we had our clashes, as all families do, but through even those, I was learning. VIPs would come to the building and secretaries would be introduced, as would other staff members. We mattered! That's when I knew empowerment had begun. These were *our* children. This was *our* office, *our* school. *We* were important, too. *We* had something to offer…. Before, I'd felt unworthy. After all, teachers have degrees. I talked to the children more and offered advice. They could see that Ms. Balint really cared! I began to greet VIPs as they entered as though I were the school's hostess. *I really was important, after all*…No longer did I ask what I should do, nor how I should do it. I began to trust that I would do it right.

Debbie titled her reflection "From Peon to Leader." She went on to explain how the idea of empowerment had spilled over into her home life and into her part-time job working with special needs children. She became more and more valuable to the school by, for example, taking over the canned food drive and becoming the school-community liaison.

I also appreciate the comments I received from Mary Gilewski, a computer aide at the Academy during my years there. (Mary is currently serving as a bilingual parent liaison.) This is what she wrote:

> Empowerment means to give or delegate official authority. Our staff was offered the opportunity to become empowered and initiate change. We were given the freedom to be creative and follow a project through on our own with minimum oversight.... Empowerment gave the staff the ability to be true participants in decisions and outcomes and take ownership of success and failures. Everyone's opinion and suggestion was valued and respected. Very few failed to live up to the high expectations that had been set.

Mary went on to talk about the values being fostered—*responsibility* and *trustworthiness, collegiality* and *caring*—and to say that "any perceived breach of these expectations caused serious concern by all."

This is such an important point. You see, many people in authority (managers in business, teachers, parents) are afraid of the idea of empowerment. After all, it means "delegating official authority." If you empower your staff, you're no longer "The Boss," the person who gives orders and controls things. Loss of control is frightening.

That's why it is so very, very important that empowerment be guided by personal character traits such as responsibility, respect, and caring. It must be supported with ongoing staff development, nurtured with frequent communication, held in place by an attitude of professionalism. And if there is ever a breach of these values, *everyone* is concerned.

Yes, if you empower your staff, you will give up that control that comes from being "The Boss." But you will gain far more than you lose. How else can you expect your staff to soar, to delight in reaching their full potential, to draw on the deepest possible wells of creativity and caring to nurture children?

## Leadership Insights

How does this idea of empowerment happen? It starts when a leader is able to cast aside his or her "I'm in charge here" attitude, realizes that others have special talents and abilities, and trusts that they can use those talents. The leader must be willing to release some of the power inherent in his or her position, in a title, and rely on the talents and powers of others to make what the group believes in become a reality.

Establishing a purpose for the group is critical, as is creating a shared vision—an image in the mind of what the future will be. Agreement on standards and codes of conduct is fundamental. The standards should be values-based, drawing on such humanistic values as respect, caring, responsibility, fairness, empathy, and honesty. And they must be applied, in very specific ways, to all the interactions within a group.

This is the framework in which empowerment develops. It is implemented not so much through words, but through ongoing and frequent communication and opportunity for people to develop, to learn new things, try new things.

# 5
## Empowerment Through Communication and Listening

*Nature gave us one tongue and two ears so we could hear twice as much as we speak.* —Anonymous

*When we listen to people, there is an alternating current, and this recharges us so that we never get tired of each other.* —Brenda Ueland

One morning early in the school year, one of the secretaries, a mother of two young children, came in late. I could see that she'd had quite a morning and was embarrassed to be so late.

Instead of a reprimand, I asked her into my office, where she immediately broke into tears. I put my arm around her and told her I understood her feelings. After all, I was a young mother once myself, and teaching at the time. I told her about one morning when I was getting a baby and two school-age children ready to leave for the day. I had finally managed to gather up everything—my books and papers, the children's schoolwork, and the paraphernalia that goes along with an infant to child care—only to discover that the toddler had sat down and taken off his high-top, lace-up shoes. I had to put everything down and start again—and I was already ten minutes late!

She laughed a little and told me about her morning, which was far more strenuous than lacing up a couple of high tops. She felt much better. I have a restroom adjacent to my office, and I told her to freshen up and then begin her work.

I was learning a lot. I was beginning to understand what it meant to be flexible and empathetic, sensitive to other people's feelings and needs. The staff needed to know that I cared about them. Staff are human too. When you demonstrate that you are aware of and care about their concerns, people will reciprocate. They will do whatever they can to help the school become a caring community for adults and students.

I encouraged staff to talk, to share their concerns—and not to stand in the corridors complaining. After all, I couldn't help solve a problem or issue if I wasn't aware of it. But just encouraging them to talk wasn't enough; we needed to create vehicles for communication to happen.

## Come On In—Let's Just Chat

During a faculty meeting, I announced the creation of CHAT sessions. The acronym stood for "Communications Helps All Teachers," and the sessions were developed to provide any staff member, regardless of his or her role, with an opportunity to meet one to one with me for frank, candid discussion of any topic the staff member selected.

A lot of people needed to talk, and individuals who wished to have such a session were asked to sign up on a sheet maintained in the office. These sessions were conducted during two days each month that had been set aside for that purpose. We would get a substitute to cover classes for thirty minutes. The schedule of individual sessions was announced in advance so teachers could plan and prepare for the substitute covering their class.

These sessions proved that listening is one of the most important characteristics of an effective leader. The way we communicate and listen to people is very important. People want to talk. They should have the opportunity to share their concerns and opinions with someone who wants to listen to them. As one teacher wrote to me years later, "Those sessions made me feel so good that people were concerned not only about my teaching, but about me as a person and my feelings."

When someone came into my office for a CHAT, I intentionally sat beside the person, not on the other side of my desk. Proximity is very important. After all, the purpose was to have an informal talk where I was the LISTENER and the staff could discuss any topic of their choice.

Confidentiality was sacred. I told everyone who had a CHAT with me that if anyone ever found out about our conversation, it would be because *they* had told them, not me. People realized that this was true, and a real, trusting, professional bond was established.

We talked about a lot of things: program scheduling, students' behavior in the cafeteria, opportunities for professional growth, personal problems, and everything else. Sometimes the employee just wanted to know how I was doing.

Staff members, instructional as well as non-instructional, could come with a complaint, but with one condition: they had to bring at least three suggested solutions to the problem they were complaining about. Complaining may make someone feel better, but it doesn't do much good. Talking about solutions is much more positive.

I realize now, from reading the reflections from former staff, how very important those CHATs were. Many wrote about how the sessions helped them deal with their feelings and fears of inadequacy. For example, Diana Laco, clearly found her first year of teaching to be very difficult. "There were many times that I became discouraged and seriously questioned my choice of teaching as a career," she wrote. Her reflection went on to recall the session in which I explained that many first–year teachers had the same experience and gave some examples from my own experience. She concluded by paying me the highest possible compliment: "I feel that whatever success I have achieved as a teacher is due in large part to the leadership provided by Mrs. Aranha."

Richard Birecree, a math resource teacher, simply had this to say: "We would have CHAT sessions where you could go to the office and talk about anything that was on your mind. It made me feel so good that people were concerned, not only about my teaching, but about me as a person and my feelings."

The CHAT sessions seeded their own innovations. On one occasion, an elementary instructional assistant came in to talk about the cafeteria. He had attended a workshop on lunch scheduling, and he said that a rotation lunch period might reduce crowding. He described the rotation concept, which scheduled grade levels to come to the cafeteria every fifteen minutes and stay thirty minutes for lunch. We adopted this concept. It worked. The cafeteria wasn't nearly as crowded.

Eventually, we renamed the cafeteria the Benjamin Foulois Traditional Academy Restaurant—or BFTA Restaurant for short. Teachers and students collaboratively developed rules for proper cafeteria behavior. These rules had to be followed in the BFTA Restaurant just as you would in any restaurant. Relating school behavior to what's expected in a real restaurant caught students' interests, and we were able to provide skills that they could transfer and use in society.

On another occasion, a physical education teacher expressed his concern over the lack of parental involvement at our school awards programs. Essentially, his suggestion was that we begin holding the awards program for both our primary and intermediate grades on one day, rather than over a two-day period. That way, parents with students in both grade levels would not have to take two days off from work. The teacher came to me with a plan he had developed cooperatively with his colleagues for implementation of this change. As a result, we held our awards program in the gym with 821 students. There was an increase in parental attendance—and a commendation and thanks from parents for adopting this new schedule.

Interestingly, parents became more involved in other school activities—perhaps because they sensed that the school cared about them, about their time, and about their children.

The CHATs also helped me learn. At one of our staff meetings, I had communicated that everyone did not have lesson plans available for my perusal when I visited the classrooms. All staff knew that this was expected. During a subsequent CHAT session, Scott, the special education coordinator, spoke to me honestly. He told me that teachers were really trying to do what was expected, and several had shared their concerns with him. He suggested that instead of addressing the entire staff about this particular deficit, I should call individuals in separately.

He was right. After all, when the majority of staff were following procedures, doing the right thing, it wasn't fair or appropriate to raise an issue with all of them. It reminded me of how we should work with our students in the classroom: if only a few of them are misbehaving, we shouldn't punish the entire class. How could I have forgotten such a simple principle!

This is another example of how teachers felt empowered to share concerns with me. We all were leaders and learners.

In turn, staff members were to model the same kind of listening, flexibility and empathy as they worked with their students and the students' parents. They were to provide communication time privately, and as a group, if necessary. We always communicated and remembered our purpose: we cared about children; children were why we were there; all decisions were made with the children or child in mind first. All parents and staff knew this purpose.

## Listening Works Both Ways

The open and frank communication in the CHAT sessions made it much easier to deal with some of the personnel problems that came up that first year. When we take time to show an interest in and listen to staff, they in turn will listen to us. An incident that happened later in the year proved this point.

I was in the office one afternoon when one of the teachers came to me and shared that a teacher was so angry with me about a decision I had made that she had left her room and was going home. (These situations happen in school.) She was a first-year teacher who had an altercation with a student, and she was upset that I had not suspended the student.

After sending someone to cover the class, I asked the teacher see me before leaving. The teacher was still very upset when she arrived. I asked her to compose herself and told her that she needed to listen to what I had to say. We went over the incident. I reminded her that I had listened to her describe what had happened, had listened to the student and was scheduling a parent-teacher and student conference. However, I did not believe that the circumstances warranted suspending the child.

I also talked about professionalism and liability under these circumstances. I pointed out that you never leave students unsupervised and that as an employee, no matter what your job, you just don't walk away. I shared the consequences of that.

She heard what I had to say, and she realized that her behavior and comments to the student were inappropriate for a teacher who really cared and wanted to help students achieve their best. I also told her that if she needed a day to compose herself so that she would be in the best frame of mind to teach children, I would approve her leave request.

She took my advice and upon returning, conferenced with me. We went over some alternative ways to dialogue with students and some professional standards for her as well. She told me she had talked with her university undergraduate supervisor and her mother. They had shared the same things I had discussed with her.

This particular teacher came back to teach the rest of the year. Later she took a leave of absence to get her Master's Degree. She returned to our school and became one of the most professional educators I know. Whenever I see her, she gives me a hug and says "Thank you." As a leader it is important to have the ability to deal with the emotions of others, yet continue to lead.

## Visibility, Evaluation and Feedback

Why do so many teachers become frightened when it's time for their observation? Classroom observations, along with the conferencing and feedback that occur afterwards, are the best possible opportunities for communication! Yet so many teachers dread that moment when an administrator walks in, sits down, and starts watching.

The anxiety likely comes from not understanding the purposes of the observation and not knowing what to expect as a result. I told our teachers, "Don't plan a special lesson for me. Plan special lessons every day for the students. I will observe to find your strengths and weaknesses. I will support you by providing training and resources for your weaknesses and by helping you build on your strengths. I want you to be successful."

Preparation meetings included information on what was expected in instructional delivery. We discussed the elements of effective lesson plans as well as classroom management strategies, and we distributed pre-observation planning forms. Everyone knew what to expect—during the observation and in the conferences that would follow—and their expectations could be summed up in one word: *support.*

We have all heard about principals sitting in a teacher's classroom and observing for five to ten minutes, then walking away without any constructive feedback. Perhaps you have talked with teachers who said their principals had not visited their classrooms for an entire year. Yet they had received evaluations!

If we expect people to be their best, then we must spend time not only observing, but also conferencing and providing constructive feedback and resources. In our building, all the teachers—100 percent—participated in an observation by the end of the first semester. This was a goal I set for myself. All non-tenured teachers received another formal observation during the second semester. After each observation, we scheduled a conference to provide oral and written feedback. In addition, informal observations were part of my daily travels through the school.

It is very important that new teachers have successful experiences as they enter the field. When I was a first-year teacher, I worked under a principal who made it a practice *not* to give new teachers students who were known to have behavior problems. I did the same for our new teachers. In addition, the grade level chairpersons served as mentors for the new teachers, and the new teachers met with me individually and as a group for consultation and support. I shared some of my personal experiences with them and did everything I could to encourage and support their efforts. I told them, that like everything else, the more experiences they had, the better teachers they would become. The key was to care about children, have high expectations for them, and to plan motivating lessons.

If we want to keep our best teachers, then we must make sure, with no excuses, they have the appropriate support. We must provide them with what they need to be successful.

We are losing excellent teachers because these elements are missing. Visibility, ongoing feedback and evaluation are absolute essentials!

## Leadership Insights

So much has been said and written about the importance of *listening,* yet so few people set aside special times and places where they can listen in a meaningful way to the people around them. Communications between administrators and staff, as well as among staff, must be open and frank—with opportunities to really talk and listen. This won't happen by itself—leaders must dedicate time and space for it to happen.

Visibility is equally important. Staff member like to see their leaders in their classroom and in the corridors. Visibility shows that the leader is interested and supportive, that he or she cares about what's going on. Leaders need to set their personal rituals for making themselves visible—by greeting people in the morning, by walking around during the day, by stopping by for observations and visits. How can they understand what's happening if they stay in their offices all day!

# 6

## A Community of Learners

*It is only as we develop others that we permanently succeed.*
—Harvey S. Firestone

*The moment you stop learning, you stop leading.*
—Rick Warren

Ongoing staff development was another key to our success. I had asked teachers at the beginning of the year to set aside the second and fourth Wednesdays of each month for faculty meetings. Usually we had at least one such meeting a month, with ample notice if a meeting was cancelled or rescheduled.

Sometimes, the meetings gave opportunity for teachers to vent their frustrations. At one venting session, a first grade teacher expressed her anger with a parent of a student she had been meeting with. The student had admitted taking some erasers, but the parent repeatedly told the teacher that the student had not taken them. The teacher became so upset at the meeting she broke down crying.

The staff looked at me to see my reaction. I told her that I knew how she felt, and at times I'm sure I felt like doing the same thing—as did many of the rest of the staff. Staff immediately began to acknowledge this feeling. I sat back and observed as the staff took over. The computer aide offered to set up time for the student to work on the computer. The librarian said she would allow the student time in the library. The special education coordinator agreed to work with the teacher to develop some discipline strategies appropriate for the circumstances.

This is a fine example of teachers collaborating and helping each other. It turned out to be a great meeting. This incident was not something discussed the next day or throughout the week. You see, this is what a school community is all about. We addressed a problem and we solved it collectively. We were changing the culture of the school; this was the way we did things at our school. Staff members began to care about one another. This extended throughout our daily operation.

The purpose of faculty meetings was to provide staff development training, dispense information, and to motivate and inspire everyone. It was a time to come together to talk as a group, to work together as a group.

At the beginning of the school year, I surveyed staff to obtain their ideas regarding areas of desired training. Occasionally, we brought in experts from the field for the training, and sometimes I would do the training myself. The majority of the training, however, was provided by staff members. Staff respected the talents of their colleagues.

For example, the special education teachers had excellent strategies for working with discipline problems. Many of the regular classroom teachers were having problems. Some of their students were exhibiting some of the same behaviors as our special education students, even though the students did not qualify for special placement. A team of special education teachers prepared and presented strategies to assist teachers in handling inappropriate student behavior, including use of contracts. The team presented examples of scenarios and provided handouts. They even offered to meet and provide further direct assistance to teachers—before school, after school or during planning time.

The atmosphere was one of collegiality as teachers constantly worked cooperatively, discussing their craft. Staff felt connected to each other and successful in their work. There was a sense of caring and inclusiveness throughout our school community.

Many of these meetings were training meetings in which small groups met and worked cooperatively, with a staff member acting as leader. The groups worked on a variety of concerns, like weekly block planning, setting up a role book correctly or writing professional yet precise comments on students' report cards.

From time to time, these meetings became opportunities for staff to vent their anger or frustrations, as the example cited earlier shows. I felt this was a great opportunity for me as a leader to practice my skill of being able to handle my mood, at the same time modeling to staff how to conduct themselves in conflict situations. We all needed to practice good social skills together as a group.

The trust and bonding that developed among staff, the relationships which were strengthened definitely contributed to that feeling of connectedness. Staff development promoted a caring community.

Staff meetings cannot and should not be just a series of announcements about a forthcoming parent teacher meeting, patrol activity or an assembly. They should be beneficial to staff. Also, they must be conducted in a manner that is motivating and inspirational. Staff should want to come to meetings. It was expected that everyone would be attentive; not grading papers, talking or balancing their checkbook.

Teachers would arrive for our meetings on time. They would be talking, but the minute I walked down the five steps to the media center where the meetings were held, you could hear a pin drop. I really respected them for that. Once, a high school content supervisor attended one of our meetings. Later she told me how very impressed and stunned she was since no one was grading papers or going in and out of the room. I told her we were professional, respected each other and this was a part of our behavior when attending meetings.

Caring and respect do not automatically accompany leadership. They must be earned by letting people know that you respect them, all the time—when you are meeting with them, when they're talking, when they're doing their jobs, and so on. If you talk about things like caring and respect, describe your expectations and then model them, they will happen.

## Leadership Insights

The two little quotations at the beginning of this chapter have a lot of implications. The first, by Harvey S. Firestone, states that "It is only as we develop others that we permanently succeed." If a leader does everything by himself or herself, the followers may learn a little by watching—but not enough to do the task on their own. If the leader develops others in the process of completing a task, he or she well have created colleagues who themselves can become leaders.

The second quotation says that "The moment you stop learning, you stop leading." That statement probably has a corollary that reads something like, "The moment your followers see that you have stopped learning, they will stop also—stop learning, that is, and possibly stop following also."

Learning is one of the most satisfying and joyful of human experiences. When leaders and followers are joined together in learning, you can feel the excitement.

# 7

# A Community of Cooperation—
# Leaders and Learners Working Together

*The man who gets the most satisfactory results is not always the man with the most brilliant single mind, but rather the man who can best coordinate the brains and talents of his associates.*

—W. Alton Jones

*The ultimate leader is one who is willing to develop people to the point that they eventually surpass him or her in knowledge and ability.*

—Fred A. Manske, Jr.

If you walked through the building on any given day, you might see the secretaries pitching in to help one another with a task or giving caring assistance or advice to a student. During their planning time, teachers would collaborate on teaching and classroom management strategies—each person switching from leader to learner as needed.

In time our titles and formal job descriptions meant less and less. Our school community was made up of teachers, trainers, learners and leaders. The roles were interchangeable, and everyone was expected to play each of the roles as needs arose—a learner in one situation, a leader in another, a trainer in still another.

Students, too, became leaders and helped nurture others. For example, Jan McKillen, a special needs teacher, partnered her students with Ms. Laco's kindergarten students. The special needs students became "reading buddies" for the kindergartners. It was wonderful to watch these two adult teachers collaborate, but even more wonderful to watch the special needs students become "teachers," assisting the younger ones in reading and story telling. It was phenomenal! Both levels benefited academically—and you could actually see the self-esteem growing in each special needs student as they helped a reading buddy.

We provided the staff with numerous and continuous opportunities to expand and alter their roles and take on completely new roles. In a period of two years, staff members provided training in over twenty topics: The Writing Process, Student Portfolios, Higher Level Questioning and Thinking Skills, Cooperative Learning, Assertive Discipline, Record Keeping, Grade Books, Writing Weekly and Daily Plans, Citizenship, The Amazing Brain, and Problem Solving.

All this switching between leader and follower, teacher and learner, was something like what happens when a flock of geese migrate. (See box, facing page). Like the geese, we all knew, instinctively, where we were headed, and we stuck together as a group. As the head goose, I often enjoyed falling back in the formation and being carried along by a new lead person's enthusiasm. Along with the others, I honked encouragement to the "point goose" loud and clear.

These activities had a ripple effect, extending beyond the walls of our school. For example, a group of primary teachers received training in what is called "progressive questioning," then helped to produce a videotape showing this technique at work in the classroom. Subsequently, this videotape was shown at the 1993 National Council for Teachers of Mathematics' national convention.

At the request of the county mathematics supervisor, several teachers served as "trainers of trainers" to help implement the county's new mathematics program. After receiving this training, elementary instructional assistants and teacher specialists in other schools served as trainers for their co-workers.

I can't possibly explain what this professional growth opportunity meant to some of our staff. Rather than even try, I'll let one of the math teachers, Richard Birecree, explain in his own words. (I should note that in 1998 Richard was chosen to be included in *Who's Who Among America's Teachers,* an honor we helped him celebrate.) The story appears on the next pages.

Even more things happened. A kindergarten teacher assisted in revising the county's primary project and a third grade teacher played an important role in revising the county's social studies curriculum. Many staff members taught courses in Early Childhood Education, Professional Ethics, English as a Second Language and Special Education at colleges and universities in the local area.

I had to keep up with my staff—not an easy task, considering everything that was going on. I taught graduate courses on Teacher Expectation-Student

## Lessons from the Geese

There is an interdependence in the way geese function.

*Fact*: As each bird flaps its wings, it creates an "uplift" for the bird following. By Flying in a "V" formation, the whole flock adds 71% greater flyer range than if each bird flew alone.

*Lesson*: People who share a common direction and sense of community can get where they are going quicker and easier because they are traveling on the thrust of one another.

*Fact*: Whenever a goose falls out of formation, it suddenly feels the drag and resistance of flying alone. It quickly gets back into formation to take advantage of the "lifting power" of the bird immediately in front.

*Lesson*: If we have as much sense as a goose, we will stay in formation with those who are headed in the direction we want to go.

*Fact*: When a goose gets tired it rotates back into the formation and another goose flies at the point position.

*Lesson*: It pays to take turns during the hard tasks and sharing leadership—people as with geese are interdependent with each other.

*Fact*: The geese in formation honk from behind to encourage those up in front to keep up their speed.

*Lesson*: We need to make sure our "honking" from behind is encouragement, not something less helpful.

*Fact*: When a goose gets sick or wounded or shot down, two geese drop out of formation to follow him down to protect him. They stay with him until he is either able to fly again or dies. Then they launch out on their own with another formation or catch up with their flock.

*Lesson*: If we have as much sense as the geese, we will stand by each other.

—Source unknown.

Achievement, Group Dynamics, Preventing Teacher Burnout and Implementing a Comprehensive Character Education Process.

I have learned through observation that, when you model what you communicate and expect, it will become contagious. You see, many adults—even teachers—can get so wrapped up in day-to-day hubbub that they forget how much satisfaction can be gained from learning something new and applying it. When teachers themselves are experiencing the joy of learning, it shows in everything they do. Children sense the difference.

*How can we expect children to enjoy learning if their teachers have forgotten how to learn? Think about that idea for a moment, then push it one step*

## Becoming More Than Just a Classroom Teacher
### *Richard Birecree*

My first year at Benjamin Foulois was very different from my private school teaching experience. Different, meaning that I felt like part of a team. Everyone at Foulois worked together to accomplish not only individual goals, but team goals as well.

I had a degree in business education, and my strength obviously was in teaching math. I felt comfortable and knowledge-able, but at first the teaching was difficult. Having to combine teaching skills with classroom management skills was almost too much. There were times that I thought I wouldn't teach more than one or two years.

Then everything changed. In my third year of teaching, I was appointed math coordinator for the school. This one appoint-ment probably did more for my confidence than anything up to that point. Not only was I growing as a professional and as a person, but my confidence was building as well. During the next two to three years, I would have frequent visitors in my classroom, observing my lessons. At first, this made me uncomfortable, but with time each instruction period became just another math lesson.

It was in the spring of 1994 that I really started to feel like more than just a regular classroom teacher. Along with two other teachers, I was invited to give a demonstration lesson to the vice-principals in the county. Although the three of us were very nervous, we were excited for the opportunity. We knew this would be our chance to show other administrators our strengths. Up to this point, teachers within our building—people I knew—would come to my classroom to observe lessons, look at how I set up lesson plans, and ask for general techniques in teaching math. The demonstration lessons, however, were something new. We would be outside our building, standing in front of strangers.

Throughout the next few years, I became more and more confident in my abilities as a math teachers. I felt as if I was empow-ered not only to teach students but also to assist teachers as well. I began doing in-service training during our regularly scheduled staff meetings, in addition to helping teachers plan and teach math

*continued on next page...*

*continued from previous page...*

lessons. I felt like I was becoming an important member of the school team and the community. I found myself staying after school to assist students with their math work as well as just talking and building their confidence—just as my co-workers had done for me earlier in my career.

In the fall of 1998, Benjamin Foulois was awarded a challenge grant from the state of Maryland. Each challenge school was asked to have one person serve as "Challenge Resource Teacher." I accepted the position, but with one regret: I would no longer have my own classroom.

Life was very different. First, I was asked to give a presentation at our meeting of cluster schools. Next, I began to present at math workshops and even taught first and second year teachers at a summer math institute. In October of 2000, I was asked to be a presenter at the annual Maryland Council of Teachers of Mathematics conference in Suitland, Maryland. I gladly accepted. I was beginning to realize there was a whole different part of education outside the classroom, a part that I never knew existed. I saw that I could make a world of difference—even if I was not in the classroom.

To this day, I have teachers calling me daily for advice on teaching mathematics. Parents call to ask for ideas and programs they can use at home. Supervisors and administrators ask me to give workshops on methods and teaching techniques.

I was recently speaking with a former student who is now a senior in high school. She is doing very well and has already been accepted at a number of very prestigious universities. When I asked her what she wanted to study in college, she responded with "I want to be a math teacher because of you."

After our conversation, I began to think of all the people who had worked hard to make me a successful teacher, and, as a result, what I was able to do to make her a successful student. I think she wants to be a math teacher because of *all* the positive experiences she had during her time at Benjamin Foulois—not just the time she sat in my class. I just happened to be her fifth and sixth grade teacher. I was able to guide her through two difficult grades and expose her to all the possibilities that a good education and a positive attitude can create—just as people earlier had done for me.

*further. How can we expect teachers to enjoy learning if their principal and others in authority have forgotten how to learn?*

Actually, this idea applies to all leaders—in schools, homes, and communities. Recall Rick Warren's advice, cited earlier, that "The moment you stop learning, you stop leading." How true!

## Learning to Measure Success

Our superintendent, Dr. John Murphy, made it a priority to provide principals with ongoing staff development and training. We were thoroughly trained in effective school research during my tenure at Benjamin Foulois. These research techniques, developed by Ron Edmonds and Larry Lezotte, gave us the statistical tools to measure the effectiveness of our work. It was expected that we include these correlates in our individual School Improvement Plans. For some principals, the project may have appeared daunting at first. After hearing presentations on the techniques, we received huge handbooks containing articles, information and procedures about implementing this process. Using these professional research techniques on our own work added to our professionalism.

These seven correlates served as a framework for our school's success:
1. A safe and orderly environment
2. Opportunity to learn on time and on task
3. Instructional leadership
4. Frequent monitoring of students
5. Clear and focused mission
6. Climate of high expectations for success for all students
7. Positive home-school relations

This was it in a nutshell. After learning all about it, I returned to the school to explain and train the staff in these correlates.

Our staff development and leadership program continued throughout the school year. We conducted monthly meetings with the School Based Management Team (SBMT) to monitor and evaluate our School Improvement Plan. The entire staff had opportunity to provide input for the plan and received copies of it. Every teacher was a member of, or was directly represented by, a fellow teacher on this team. Every staff member (whether certified or not) had an opportunity to be creative and share a wealth of knowledge and suggestions for the continued improvement of our school. Our school environment articulated, fostered and protected our central school value that we were a community of leaders and learners and staff developers.

There's no use in providing training if one doesn't use it. You must ensure the application and use of the training.

Our next step was to develop our school improvement plan based on our mission and purpose, and on our dedication and commitment to what we wanted to accomplish for our students. We developed a strategic plan. We set goals, objectives and strategies, and we allocated resources. And we included a plan for evaluating our work. We monitored the plan and remained flexible, making any changes determined to be necessary.

Under Dr. Murphy's administration, principals were also trained in School Based Instructional Management and Decision Making. Sometimes I took key staff to meetings with me so that I could share these creative and helpful techniques.

Frequently, leaders will say they don't have the time for learning. Isn't that sad? We must *make* the time. There was no such word as "can't" in our vocabulary. You see, when you make the time for staff development and training, the staff, students, parents and you will benefit. You will even have more time to be that important head leader with a purpose.

We made it a point to provide the staff with a wealth of professional literature and articles. If I read an article and thought that the ideas expressed would be beneficial, I would put the article in the teachers' mailboxes and ask them to read it by the next faculty meeting. Sometimes, I assigned an article to all teachers of a certain grade level and asked them to make a presentation, based on the article, at the next staff meeting. Also, we established a professional library in a small area in the media center. Staff members could check out media, books, videos and magazines for their classroom or professional use.

Ongoing staff development for principals and staff is absolutely necessary for school improvement. I can't emphasize this strongly enough.

## Learning from the Parents

As part of our leadership development, we solicited input from parents. Open house night was a great opportunity to set up a dialogue with parents as a group. As is true for most schools, the open house was a time when the majority of parents would be together in one place. I would dismiss the teachers to their rooms and take the remaining time to discuss our mission and purpose. I encouraged parents to work with our administration and to focus on bringing out the best in their children.

As a follow-up, we sent a survey home to the parents, seeking their input regarding areas of need, where the school could provide assistance and guidance. The school administration also identified certain areas warranting special attention based on our expertise and professional observations. After compiling the areas of need from these two sources (parental surveys and the school's list), we set priorities and planned for a fall and spring mini conference for parents. Staff and outside resource personnel conducted sessions on a variety of topics developed from the two sources.

The conferences were held at night. Parents were able to attend at least two different sessions. We held a drawing during this event. Some of the rewards were furnished from our business community or from businesses run by the students' parents. Sessions addressed topics like the new math, improving self-esteem, assisting students with homework and managing conflict and anger.

Our parent teacher meetings sometimes involved "talking circles." Groups of parents would share similar problems and experiences with their children. These circles were great opportunities for our parents to connect with, even mentor, each other. This activity increased parental involvement in the school, and also improved student/parent relationships.

Parental mentoring and training became an important part of the school's culture. Parents were visible and welcomed in our school, and over time they became members of our community of leaders.

## People Want to Help—Let Them

You see, people *want* to have input in helping to achieve an organization's goals. They must be given the opportunity, autonomy and trust to do so. At the same time, they must be allowed to take risks. If they fail, there should be no blame. Failure is a way of learning. Many times we become more successful at what we do after failure. I once read that "There's only one way to fail and that's to quit." Both adults and students need this message communicated to them—and communicated repeatedly As with the staff, I often provided parents with motivational literature. The poem on the facing page provides one example.

## Be a Winner

If all around you are quitting, as they sometimes do
If your critics are many and friends are few
If obstacles confront you at every turn
Remember the lessons that winners learned....

To stop and quit you will never win
Until you decide to try it again.
When life's little hurdles slow you down,
Just steady your pace and hold your ground.

Hold fast to your dreams, as they can come true
When you do the best that you can possibly do.
To win you must believe that you will not fail.
Perseverance is the breeze that fills your sail.

Although the unexpected may rock your boat,
Winners will weather the storm remaining afloat.
Conceive it, believe it, and know that you can
Continue step by step according to plan.
Stand up and be counted so that the world will see
That you believe in becoming the best you can be.
Accept the challenges of life and you'll continue to find
That winning is the spirit of living
...it's merely a state of mind

—Mychal Wynn

The poem "Be A Winner" was reprinted from the book, *Don't Quit: Inspirational Poetry,* by Mychal Wynn, copyright 1990, revised 1997, ISBN 1-880463-26-1. Permission granted on January 16, 2002 from the publisher, Rising Sun Publishing, Inc., P.O. Box 70906, Marietta, GA. 30007 (800) 524-2813.

# 8

## The Power of Recognition

*Educators often develop a kind of survival mentality. They ask themselves, "What can I do to just get through the day?" They go through the motions. Sometimes they withdraw to their individual classroom. The only deposits to their emotional bank account come from within the classroom walls. They feel unappreciated and undervalued. Many administrators feel the same way. One of the deepest hungers of the human soul is to be appreciated, to be valued, to be recognized. So little of this is taking place. Consequently this negative cycle feeds upon itself, intensifies, and develops it own momentum.*

—Steven Covey, Principle-Centered Leadership

A bus broke down one winter afternoon, and I had to wait at school until we made sure every student was safe on another bus. One of the staff members was aware of the incident, and he came to my office. He offered to stay with me as long as needed, and to assist in notifying parents to tell them why their children would be late. I told him that his offer was very thoughtful, but the task had been completed, then added, "Thanks for *all* you do!"

That evening at home, the phone rang. It was the staff member calling to say that in his sixteen years in education, no administrator had ever told him "thanks for all you do." He just wanted to let me know how much that meant to him.

*Can you believe that? This man had been a teacher for sixteen years, and never once had an administrator thanked him for all he had done!*

Everyone needs to feel appreciated and acknowledged sometime. When adults or children do well or accomplish a goal or mission that's been established,

63

appropriate recognition *should* be given. It doesn't have to be a monetary award. We found ways to recognize staff, students and parents at our school—individuals as well as teams—and the most meaningful recognition didn't cost us a dime! How much does it cost to give a handshake or hug, or to say "thank you" and really mean it!

It's important to know your employees, of course. Some people love being singled out and placed in the spotlight; others prefer to share their expertise, but shun any public acknowledgment. This is where the CHAT sessions were beneficial. One employee, for example, shared some excellent math resource material and strategies for improving students' math skills. She asked, however, not to be singled out for any recognition. I found a way to recognize her by including her in a team award. Later, she commented to me, "Thanks—you're really something else." The team award was the right way to reward her—it let her know how deeply we appreciated her efforts without making her feel self-conscious.

Like the staff member who offered to help that day when the bus broke down, teachers and others often told me how nice it was to feel appreciated. This idea came up repeatedly in the reflections on life at Benjamin Foulois I received from former staff members. For example, Lori Carluccio, who taught a fifth/sixth-grade combination class, emphasized that the recognitions had given her the confidence to be more creative in her teaching. When a new program to help students raise test scores was implemented, she rushed to my office, eager to learn how to apply these "exciting new initiatives and teaching methods." Eventually, she found herself speaking to groups of administrators and teachers about the methods she had learned. "This was something I was generally not comfortable with," she wrote. "But Mary, you believed I could do it, *and made me believe in myself as well.*"

Lori is currently mothering two young sons. "I have taken what I learned and applied it to my life as a wife, mother, daughter, and friend," she wrote. "I try to let my own children know how much I care about them and how special they are to me each and every day.... I try to model good behavior in our home and in our community. I have the confidence to lead by example, in no small part thanks to the example set at the Benjamin Foulois Academy."

There's one other story I want to share. It comes from Jan McKillen, formerly a special education teacher at the school. In writing out the story for me, she emphasized that the ability to "recognize each individual student's strengths, contributions, and accomplishments" was that hidden force that made her efforts a success. I find the story (see box, facing page) deeply touching.

64

## Ronnie's Story

I had been teaching for several years when I became aware of Ronnie. Ronnie was a fourth-grade, regular education student who had not yet been identified as a special needs student and subsequently did not qualify for special education services. Stories of his daily exploits were well-documented and shared by teachers and students alike. Among other behaviors, he frequently launched verbal attacks on our special education students, calling them "retards." So, on the day my coordinator informed me that for the remaining two months of the school year, Ronnie would be joining our class, my first action was to call a class meeting.

Many of my students had been targets of Ronnie's abuse, and their initial reaction to having Ronnie in our class was less than positive. As always, everyone shared his/her concerns. After much discussion and some effective role-playing to experience life from Ronnie's perspective, the class unanimously agreed to forgo our preconceived impressions of Ronnie and welcome him into our class. Two of our more patient students volunteered to act as buddies, to help Ronnie with as smooth a transition as possible.

When the day came for Ronnie's first appearance, he was MIA—missing in action.. After a thorough search, we discovered him hiding in the boys' bathroom, determined to avoid the inevitable. After some prolonged and intense coaching, he reluctantly appeared. One by one, students introduced themselves and shared a favorite class activity. Ronnie's response made me smile, his eyes growing wide with surprise as he listened to students' accounts of swimming, bowling, roller-skating, cooking lessons, science fair projects, and "hole in-one," a game where teams shot baskets after giving correct answers to math and language questions.

The Ronnie we grew to know was entirely different from that kid with a "bad rep" we had heard so much about. Not only did Ronnie learn to read in those last two months of school, but, thanks to his newly found self-esteem, he, too, became a role model who looked for the good in others.

He made new friends, *the best of whom was himself.*

—Jan McKillen

The form of the recognition for staff members varied. Sometimes it was simply a handshake, a smile or a hug. At other times it was a statement such as "I'm glad you're here!" On some occasions, a letter or note was placed in the staff member's mailbox: "You've earned lunch with the principal. I'll drive!" or "You have earned a half-day planning time: see the secretary to make arrangements for a substitute."

You know, in view of the many demands people have in their lives, the simple gift of *time* can be precious indeed.

Teachers need opportunity to network, plan and dialogue—and giving them this opportunity is itself a form of recognition. Sometimes, we called in two or three substitutes for an entire day. This arrangement made it possible for teachers from two different grade levels to have half days for planning and sharing, one group of teachers in the morning and a different group in the afternoon. These teachers had an opportunity to discuss instructional strategies, classroom management, and other concerns. I was impressed by the strong sense of collegiality that these meetings fostered.

During my daily visits to classrooms, I would take note of teachers' instructional delivery and their interaction with students. Many teachers do a great job in their instructional delivery—and so much of it goes unrecognized! What a shame! In one case, a teacher had taught all of the students to respond to questions in complete sentences. This type of oral communication helped students with their writing skills.

I knew that instructional techniques like this needed to be shared—but how? After some reflection, we created a new program called "Feature Teacher of the Week." I would use the public address system to describe the great instructional activities I had observed in a particular classroom. Staff members were encouraged to visit the "Feature Teacher's" classroom to see for themselves. The instructional activities might be effective teaching practices, exemplary classroom management, bulletin board displays, group projects, or anything else that other teachers could learn from.

This sharing of activities led, in turn, to another program. Teachers who displayed a high level of expertise volunteered to serve as role models and mentors for their colleagues. These mentor teachers invited new teachers to visit their classrooms as observers and provided in-service training at faculty or staff development meetings. You see, for teachers (and for many others), the opportunity to play the role of mentor is in itself a high form of recognition.

It's amazing how even a few words of recognition can make a difference. In her reflections about life at Benjamin Foulois, Doreen Kowall-Harris, formerly a sixth grade teacher, refreshed my memory of an incident that I had all but forgotten. I had been taking a new staff member on a building tour, and I introduced the new person to Doreen by saying, "Here is a master teacher I would like you to meet."

"It was then that I realized you were speaking of *me,* a somewhat inexperienced first-year teacher," Doreen wrote in her note to me. She went on to recall that I often referred to her as a master teacher in the presence of others. "I never understood why you did that," she confessed. "However, the compliments helped to create a sense of self-confidence that enabled me to become a better teacher and to explore how I could expand on the qualities that a master teacher possesses."

Of course, my comments to her were not casual or insincere. As an experienced educator, I could see the "master teacher" developing in her long before she was aware of her potential. My perception was accurate. Doreen is currently an elementary school principal in Penn Hills, Pennsylvania. Based on reports I hear, her leadership is outstanding.

In addition to "Feature Teacher of the Week," we created an "Employee of the Month" award. I decided to do this after observing the plaques displayed in two Giant Food stores located in Prince George's County. During separate meetings with each of the store managers, I learned their procedure for selecting the employee. I was impressed by how each of these managers took the time to meet with me and explain in detail how their program operated. You see, I didn't make any appointment to see them. I simply walked in and asked for help—and they provided it.

Their information gave us ideas for implementing our version of the Employee of the Month program. Initially, I talked to the staff about the methods for recognition, to get some of their ideas. It became clear that, under no circumstances, was the award to be based on an individual's popularity. Employees were to select prospective employees of the month based on leadership, professionalism, collegiality and other character traits. I emphasized to the staff that I trusted their judgment and that the administrators would not be involved in the selection.

This is how it worked. Staff members selected the Employee of the Month using a secret ballot procedure. In addition to teachers and teaching assistants, all food service personnel, building maintenance employees and clerical services employees were eligible to vote for—and to be selected as—the Employee of the Month. Individual employees who were selected had their names engraved on a plaque prominently displayed in the front entrance hall of our school. Also, they had exclusive use of a specially designated Employee of the Month parking space throughout the month of recognition.

The employee also received an automobile license tag cover stating "Employee of the Month" with the school name and month indicated on it, as well as other appropriate gifts such as flowers, a half day planning time or lunch with the principal.

Ribbons, pins, notes, buttons, plants, flowers, extra planning time, extra duplicating paper (yes, teachers especially appreciated this one!) and other supplies— served with an abundance of verbal praise—these were our methods of recognition. And each gift was a validation of who that person was, who we were and what we were accomplishing as a community.

Our students were also recognized. The administration and staff communicated to the entire student body that their school was a place of business, just like the places where their parents worked. Each student's job was to come to school to learn, study and do his or her best. This would help them pursue a career of their choice, but also learn to be good citizens. Of course, students were not rewarded for everything they did. We explained that we simply expected that they would do their jobs well—they were doing this for themselves.

However, to help students stay focused, motivated and interested in learning, we recognized and encouraged students' talents just as we had done with the faculty and staff. Each quarter we had assemblies to recognize students who had earned a place on the Principal's Honor Roll (all A's); the Academic Honor Roll (A's and B's) and the Citizenship Honor Roll (A's in study habits and behavior). Students received trophies, certificates and ribbons. A student from each class was named "Most Improved Student" in each of the content areas and creative arts areas.

We need to remember that there are a variety of known "intelligences" other than verbal and mathematical intelligence—the intelligences that show in academic work. That's why it was important to recognize talents and achievements in the creative arts and in physical education.

We learned to use many different strategies to develop positive attitudes and perceptions about learning. We validated our respect for the students by speaking positively to them, using appropriate voice tones and facial expression. We made sure that the students understood that we had high expectations for them, as students and as future citizens of the world. Children were told, "Thank you," "You've done a great job" and "We're proud of you." If a teacher or staff member made an error in dealing with a student, we cared enough to apologize to the student.

Let me make one more important point. These rewards, recognitions and acknowledgements were part of our daily life—but we all knew we had to do our jobs *without expecting to be rewarded.* Being a leader and contributing to the improvement of the school as well as the academic and social achievement of our students was just a part of our school's culture, the way we did things at our school. It was part of "Who we were" and "How we operated."

How does one evaluate the importance of praise and recognition? Each year the number of students who earned honor roll status increased from the first quarter to the fourth one. Each year teachers and staff expressed to me that they felt they had grown professionally, as well as in their human capacity to understand and nurture others. And people like Lori, Doreen, and Jan continue to remind me how important recognition was in their lives.

## Leadership Insights

You know, most people don't see themselves all that clearly, and when we help them recognize their talents, we set them on the path to developing their potential. Our recognition of another person's talents fosters self-recognition, the individual's awareness of his or her gifts. I think we are all humbled, at times, to recognize how we have been blessed with God-given talents—as well as opportunities to use those talents to help others. We should be thankful to those who helped us recognize our talents. And the most meaningful thanks we can give to those who nurtured us are to nurture others.

# 9

## The Power of Vision

*Leaders today must begin with a strong vision and a set of positive beliefs to support it; without these, the people they lead will not only lose, they'll be lost.*
—Ken Blanchard

*Without vision, the people perish.*
—Proverbs 29:18

I can remember how I used to dream about things when I was a youngster. I don't mean just *daydream.* It was more than that. I would make a clear, detailed mental picture about something. It might be something I wanted to do, something I wanted to be, somewhere I wanted to go, or something I wanted to accomplish Next came planning and not stopping until that picture in my mind *started to happen, became something that I was living.*

Back then, I didn't call it "visualizing." It was simply a matter of dreaming about something I wanted to happen, then planning.

You know, we all do something like that sometime in our lives. But how many of us take the time to make it more than a daydream, to form a really focused and detailed picture in our minds? How many of us work toward the visualization with dedication, commitment and persistence—unwilling to let obstacles or problems mess up our vision?

I attended kindergarten in public school, first through fourth grades in parochial school, and fifth and sixth grades in Birney Elementary School, a public school in Washington, DC. These schools were enjoyable places to be as well as serious learning environments. Teachers *cared* about our learning, academically as well as socially. They were *determined* that we should learn. Staff did not give up on us. We were told we had to work hard and be better than our best. This was the message from our teachers.

We didn't know it, but those teachers had a vision of what education should be and how it can affect people's lives in positive ways. No, they wouldn't have called it a vision. But they knew that to become educated was to become *respected*—by parents, school staff, students, and society in general. They didn't know what careers we would choose, but they saw us as becoming respected members of society, people who worked hard and did our best, and who used our education to make life better for ourselves and others.

They had a vision of what education can be, and a vision of what each of us could become. They passed those visions on without us even knowing what was happening!

As I reflect on my fifth and sixth grade teacher, Mrs. Jackson—oh, that was so long ago!—I truly understand the way this idea of "vision" can take hold and shape a person's life. It was in that classroom that I dreamed that I wanted to be a teacher. I visualized myself teaching children the same way Mrs. Jackson had taught us. My focus from then on was to do everything that would lead me to becoming a teacher.

Life is full of changes. Some are unexpected, others come as a product of learning and growing and assuming new roles and responsibilities. Each change creates the need for a new "vision session." When I became a principal, I knew I had to sit down and use that "vision making" part of my mind all over again. Everything depended on that.

I first visualized the kind of leader I wanted to be, then shared this vision with the staff. More importantly, I shared my mental picture of the school in which I wanted to work.

During one of our first meetings, I asked the staff to listen as I closed my eyes and described my ideal school aloud. I talked about working with adults that were professional and had a passion for assisting children to be their best. I just talked on and on, giving image after image of what I saw happening. My words were like a movie camera, taking the listeners on a tour from the front office, through the corridors, to the gym and the parking lot—image by image, detail by detail, creating a vision that we could build together and share.

Next, I asked them to listen as I visualized the interactions between the components that made up our school: the interactions between administrators and staff, staff and administrators, staff and parents, and so on. I was especially detailed in visualizing our behavior toward students. I gave examples of how we communicated with them, how we assisted them in their learning, and how we would partner with parents in working with their children.

To describe my picture of the overall school culture, I used the six "E" words in Kevin Ryan's "Six E's of Moral Education." The six key words were Ryan's, but I wrote my own explanation for each.

1. ***Example.*** As adults, we set examples.

2. ***Explanation.*** We explain to students the rationale for why we do things the way we do at our school: the discipline policy, uniform policy, attendance policy, etc. Students have input into developing policies in as many areas as possible.

3. ***Exhortation.*** We use exhortation (sparingly) in conjunction with explanation to appeal to the best instincts of our students and move them into a particular direction.

4. ***Experience.*** We provide students with opportunities to serve and help others. Students are encouraged to help teachers and other students. Older students act as mentors and tutors for younger children. Upper grade students team with lower grade students in helping them to read. Children in our school learn to appreciate differences in others by helping physically handicapped students as well as special needs students.

5. ***Environment.*** Both the physical and the human environment support learning.

6. ***Excellence of Expectation.*** We get what we expect. We have high expectations for all of our students and for ourselves. We expect the best! We go beyond the call of duty to achieve it.

I talked about what I'd like to see when I visited classrooms: current written lesson plans available for viewing (either on the desk or being used by the teachers), daily plans and objectives posted, and so on. It was clear, from the words I used, that I wasn't visualizing a quiet classroom, but one where children were interacting, responding and/or working cooperatively. I visualized the teachers motivating and inspiring young people to learn by using Direct Teaching Activities (DTA's). These include a lesson objective communicated orally and in writing, a developmental teaching lesson, a guided practice activity, an independent activity, an assessment and a closure to the lesson. I described how learning would be integrated in both the cognitive and affective domains.

I envisioned all children learning regardless of their race, religion, or socioeconomic status, regardless of whether they lived in two-parent homes, single-parents homes, or were homeless. *There were no excuses when it came to helping children learn.* I envisioned a caring staff *that simply declined to make excuses* for any student not being able to learn.

Remember that I had my eyes closed while I talked. Next it was their turn. I asked the staff to close their eyes and visualize the kind of leader *they* wanted to work with, the qualities of their work environment and their ideal school.

After a while, I asked individual staff members to respond to a set of questions about their ideal school. Everyone was eager to respond. As each person expressed his or her vision, another staff member recorded the speaker's comments on a flip chart.

Next, we reviewed and compared my vision with the visions expressed by the staff, then developed a list that merged their visions with mine. (This wasn't difficult—the lists contained essentially the same qualities.)

*The important point is this: We had developed a shared vision—a vision that was achieved collaboratively and would be made a reality by cooperation and collaboration.*

## Institutionalizing the Vision—An Ongoing Process

In the year that followed, we never let ourselves lose sight of the vision. It was articulated at every faculty meeting, individual conference and committee meeting. It was written into our handbook and verbalized at every opportunity—including our rituals and celebrations. Everyone in the school knew where we were headed. We were working toward the reality of our school becoming "A Good Place to Be."

At our first open house meeting for parents, we shared our vision and solicited their views about the kind of school they wanted their children to attend. We added these ideas to our vision. From then on, achieving the vision became our goal. We developed our school improvement plan in alignment with our vision and the school district's vision. We set goals, objectives, strategies; we allocated human, material, and financial resources; we included formative and summative evaluations that could be monitored, reflected on and modified when needed. Every staff member had a copy of this plan and the opportunity for input into the decision-making process. And every single one of these activities supported the vision.

## The Ideal Classroom

All of the foregoing was done collectively and would be achieved collaboratively. That's good, and that's the way it should be. *But that wouldn't be enough.* The power of visualization also had to take hold on an *individual* level.

To make this transition, I used information that I had received during an advanced professional workshop presented by Bill Blokker, Ed. D, entitled "Vision, Visibility, Symbols." One exercise (see box, below) guides teachers to respond to six important components in creating their classroom visions.

---

### Six components for an ideal classroom

—Academic growth of students in your ideal classroom.

—Behavioral growth of the students in your ideal classroom.

—Professional growth of the teachers in your ideal classroom.

—Interaction of people in your ideal classroom:

Student/Student; Teacher/Parent;

Teacher/Student; Student/Parent.

—Feelings which are present in your ideal classroom.

—Climate and appearance in your ideal classroom.

*Source:* Bill Blokker. Workshop presentation, "Vision, Visibility, Symbols."

---

After the teachers had an opportunity to think about these components, I asked each one to write out a vision of his or her classroom, using the components as a guide. My goodness! What concentration and creativity went into those vision statements! Some teachers wrote in outline form, others used detailed paragraphs, and one person used a "presentation format"—words arranged on a page to emphasize how ideas were connected.

You could feel the energy that went into each statement. For example, here is how Edith Weaver envisioned academic growth in her third grade classroom.

> My ideal classroom will be one in which all students achieve to their
> fullest potential. Children will be learning, not only from my
> guidance and the resources I can provide, but also from each other.
> As I glance around the room, I will see groups of children working

cooperatively to find answers—in teams, partner groups, or independently. In each setting, the children will be involved in competitive, challenging, and fun activities that will help them to reinforce their own abilities.

The idea of cooperation and partnerships was emphasized over and over in the visions. This idea didn't apply just among students, but also between parents and teacher and between parents and their children. Here, for example, is how Sandra Hansen saw interpersonal interactions in her ideal fourth grade classroom:

> Students will encourage weaker and slower peers. Help will be offered and graciously accepted among peers.
> Parents will be helping me plan their children's education. We will discuss their child's learning style and ways to improve learning. Homework will be adjusted to help each child.
> I visualize having time to really communicate with each child, to give each child individual help on their level so that they can proceed as far as possible in attaining knowledge and skill.
> The children will accept their parents as partners in their advancement, not adversaries. They would work their best to please their parents.

Here's another example, from Ann Lancaster, a first grade teacher.

> I envision a classroom where both the students and I will be eager to come each and every day….The children will work in pairs or small groups so that they can learn with and about each other. I will keep close contact with the parents through progress reports, telephone calls, and conferences. I will encourage the parents to come into the classroom and observe their child. …. Praise would be used often, as well as smiles and other rewards. I will foster good interactions between parents and children by holding conferences in which both the parents and their child are present. I will suggest activities that parents and students can do together. I want the students to feel good about themselves and their abilities. When this is accomplished, they will interact positively with each other.

In describing the feelings that would be present in their ideal classrooms, the teachers listed all of those positive emotions that support both academic and social development: feelings of acceptance, a sense of belonging, concern for each other, a realization that their teacher really cared about them. They would be excited about learning, eager for new challenges, and confident in their abilities.

In describing the climate and appearance of their ideal rooms, the teachers saw bright, neat, well organized rooms filled with colorful bulletin board displays celebrating the children's accomplishments. "It is a room that the children are proud of," one teacher wrote. "They will want to keep it neat and attractive because they are proud of it."

I was especially impressed by the way one of the special education teachers, Margaret Rees-Krebs, pictured both the feelings and the climate in her ideal classroom. Her descriptions—in the "presentation format" mentioned earlier—are reproduced below and on the following page.

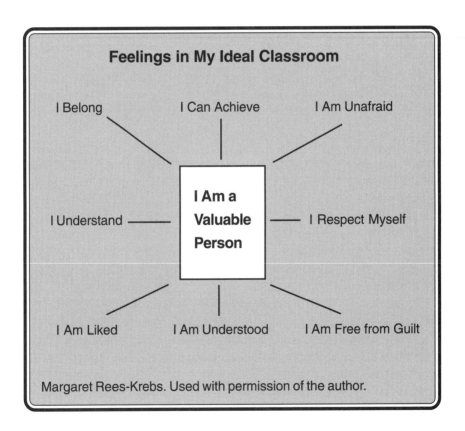

**Feelings in My Ideal Classroom**

I Belong — I Can Achieve — I Am Unafraid

I Understand — **I Am a Valuable Person** — I Respect Myself

I Am Liked — I Am Understood — I Am Free from Guilt

Margaret Rees-Krebs. Used with permission of the author.

> ## Climate in My Ideal Classroom
>
> Warmth          Enthusiasm          Anticipation
>
> Laughter          Cooperation          Concentration
>
> Support     Encouragement    Order     Fairness
>
> Excitement          Sharing          Triumph
>
> Satisfaction     Striving          Helping          Security
>
> Acceptance          Challenge     Consistency
>
> Attainment          Forgiveness          Understanding
>
> Flexibility          Appreciation
>
> Margaret Rees-Krebs. Used with permission of the author.

## Awakening Dormant Visions

I believe that everyone who enters the education profession has a picture of an ideal classroom somewhere in the back of his or her mind, and that image is probably similar to the visions these teachers wrote about. But for so many teachers, that vision is either unfocused or allowed to become dormant because of the conditions they find in their schools.

We, too, confronted many of those conditions. Recall that ours was a magnet school, and many of our students carried with them those terrible obstacles to learning that come packaged along with urban poverty. We were able to stir life into those dormant visions and make the obstacles go away.

We were able to accomplish this for several reasons. First, we started with a set of shared values. I can't emphasize that enough. Next, we created a detailed vision of how leadership would work at our school, and we collaborated to form a picture of the total school environment—the physical plant as well as the way people acted toward each other. *Then we had each individual teacher make that vision personal.* They didn't just talk about it; they really concentrated on what they wanted and they *wrote it down on paper.*

They saw their personal actions as part of a group working together. As Margaret Rees-Krebs wrote in her vision statement, "My ideal classroom is located in the ideal school with the same feelings, climate, and interactions present in the entire school that are present in this classroom."

Next, we discussed the vision statements during individual conferences and provided the support and resources needed to make each teacher's classroom vision come to life. We worked at it individually and together, always reminding each other that there were to be no excuses about why our students couldn't learn.

## Leadership Insights

There is a lesson here for leaders in all fields—business, community, volunteer service, and heads of families—to consider very seriously.

Almost all business publications on leadership emphasize the importance of vision. In business, a vision is not just as something that "makes people feel good." Rather, it focuses the energy that drives the company's financial success. Robert Knowling, CEO of Covad Communications, points out that business executives seem to enjoy writing strategies—new ways of making and selling products. He emphasizes, however, that "it is vision and values that spawn strategic action" and that "the absence of vision will doom any strategy—especially a strategy for change." He adds that "A true vision shapes your hiring, assessment, and promotion of employees, and your behavior toward customers, partners, and investors. It is a more powerful tool for leading an organization than any market analysis or spreadsheet." (Interview in *Leader to Leader,* a publication of the Peter Drucker Institute, Fall 2000).

The same is true in almost all other leadership endeavors. In schools, a vision of what the learning environment is to be should shape every aspect of the interactions among teachers, administrators, non-teaching staff, students, and parents. It should guide hiring practices, teaching assignments, and budget decisions. Without vision, any strategy—especially a strategy to change something, to make things better—is doomed to fail.

Leaders need to lead the way in setting the vision for a group, then challenge each individual to create and live a personal vision that supports the group vision. They should introduce and reinforce the premise that there are to be no excuses for compromising their visions. They should ensure that that everyone has the resources he or she needs.

Finally, they should be prepared to recognize accomplishments and celebrate successes.

# 10

## The Power of Ethical Citizenship and Character Education

*To make your children capable of honesty is the beginning of education.*
— John Ruskin

*We must remember that intelligence is not enough. Intelligence plus character. This is the true goal of education.*
—Dr. Martin Luther King

It's early on a Monday morning in November, the week of Thanksgiving, and we are ready for a new "Topic of the Week." As the public address system switches on, students in all the classes listen attentively to a scripted dialogue.

*Sarah:* Good morning, James. What's wrong?

*James:* Well, my teacher gave us an assignment to write a paper on the topic of the week, "Being thankful and showing gratitude for all we have." He wants us to elaborate on all we are thankful for.

*Sarah:* OK. So what's the problem?

*James:* The problem is that I can't think of anything that I have to be thankful for.

*Sarah:* Come on. You can't think of anything?

*James:* Nope. I didn't get the new video game I wanted last week and my parents didn't take me to Adventure World for Halloween.

81

| Sarah: | How about being thankful for a home and enough food to live on? |
|---|---|
| James: | Why should I be thankful for a home and food? |
| Sarah: | Be thankful for a home because it is where we live. It can be a house, apartment, condominium, shelter, townhouse or trailer home. A home is where you feel safe and comfortable. Someone is there to care for you, especially when you can't care for yourself. It's a place where there are people or a person who supports and guides you through life. That's truly something to be thankful for. You know, many people throughout the world don't have homes or enough food to live on. Hundreds of people die every day of starvation. |
| James: | I never thought of it like that before. I do have a lot to be thankful for. My parents work hard, and they make sacrifices to provide me with all that I need, such as a home and food. |
| Sarah: | Not only do our parents work hard to provide us with what we need, but so do teachers, our principal, school administration, cafeteria and custodial workers. People who work in our neighborhoods and communities are also there to help us. |
| James: | *(Excited)* I know a way we can show we are grateful during Thanksgiving and throughout the year! |
| Sarah: | How? |
| James: | We can be good to our parents or guardians, grandparents, school staff and our community helpers. We can treat them with kindness and give them the respect that they deserve. Or we can always say thank you in a polite, friendly manner. |
| Sarah: | Well, I better be getting to class. See ya! |
| James: | OK. Bye! |

As I listened to the dialogue, I would find myself thinking about all the ways teachers would be using the topic as part of their lesson plans during the week. What a great opportunity for creative writing in the language arts lessons! Of course, the social studies lessons would include discussion of the first Thanksgiving. But it wouldn't stop there: the topic would be incorporated into health lessons, even math and science lessons.

Scripted dialogues such as this were an essential component of the school's Ethical Citizenship and Courtesy Program. Every Monday started with an introduction to the topic of the week and provided the children with examples of specific positive behaviors associated with the topic. Each day thereafter, teachers in all the classes repeated, explained and reinforced the topic. Bulletin board displays further focused attention on the topic. More importantly, everyone in the school—staff, teachers, and students—made an effort to not only demonstrate the behaviors associated with the topic, but also to notice and reinforce those behaviors in others.

Others participated, too. When we started this program, the principal would give the topic of the week. Eventually, a teacher, a secretary, a custodian, a counselor or a parent would deliver the topic. Each month, a list of topics for the month was sent to parents via the school newsletter, and parents were encouraged to reinforce the topics at home.

The school year would begin with a topic like "Getting Off to a Good Start with Myself and My Teacher." Subsequent topics might deal with good behavior on the school bus and the playground, in the lunchroom and public places, and cover the qualities of being generous, responsible, and honest. The school year typically ended with a topic like "Being the Best During the Vacation Months." Some topics, such as self-discipline, were revisited throughout the year.

Every month, students in each classroom selected a student to be that class's Citizen of the Month. The members of the class, not the teacher, made the selection. Each Citizen of the Month received a certificate, and the student's photograph was displayed in the front hall of the school. In addition, the classes recognized their Citizens of the Month at celebrations such as a pizza or ice cream parties. Local businesses such as Shakey's Pizza, McDonald's and Tastee Freeze sometimes provided food for our citizenship parties.

As the Ethical Citizenship and Courtesy Program gained momentum, we could all feel the difference. Our school became a calm, caring environment. The feeling that "this was a safe place to learn" permeated the school. Attendance rates for staff increased. Student attendance rates and promotion rates came into line with the Maryland School Performance Assessment Program (MSPAP) standards. Discipline referrals were at a minimum and suspension rates decreased dramatically. Student test scores increased incrementally each school year and parental involvement in school matters increased as well.

It's tempting to suggest that the ethical citizenship program was the single most important component for the improvements that occurred at our school. Rather, the program was one component among many. It became the umbrella for a number of other strategies, including conflict resolution, peer mediation and an effective school improvement plan. Over a period of time, these programs became a central force in transforming the school's culture. But *programs* don't make changes happen—*people* do. The strategies were complemented by the human qualities and talents found among the staff—qualities like leadership, dedication, commitment, responsibility, enthusiasm and knowledge. These qualities enabled us to perform at levels closer to our full individual potentials.

## How the Program Started

When I first arrived at the school, staff and teachers alike told me about how disrespectful the students were at times, and they vented their feelings about dealing with students who didn't show respect. My response was to ask two pertinent questions: "Why are students acting this way? And what are we going to do about it?" Clearly, we needed to look at this problem. Finding answers to these questions would be important in transforming the culture of our school.

We needed to start by reflecting on the verbal and non-verbal messages we were sending children as we interacted with them. Second, we needed to see through those disrespectful behaviors and speak to the child, the young human being in need of love and self-respect, hiding behind the attitude.

We decided to implement the Ethical Citizenship and Courtesy program as part of our effective school plan. The program would be based on the core values that guided us as a staff, but the children would be involved too. All staff would be models and living examples of those core values—and we would expect the same from our students.

As its name suggests, the Ethical Citizenship and Courtesy Program was a dual construct focused on positive values related to both character and citizenship. The program was built on central human values that virtually everyone treasures: self-respect, kindness and consideration, common forms of politeness, respect for others' property and a sense of personal responsibility—all geared toward the elementary and middle school student. (Clearly, these strategies could be modified for high school as well.)

We found that a program of instruction directed at both citizenship and courtesy skills serves a number of purposes. It provides a common language for behavioral and interpersonal skills, defines a set of shared values and goals, and explicitly articulates expectations to students and parents.

In building the program, we drew on two resources:

• We called our program The Ethical Citizenship and Courtesy Program, based on *The Good Citizenship and Courtesy Program* (1999) authored by Dr. Anne Lyons, formerly a school principal in Minnesota, and

• *Educating for Character: How Our Schools Can Teach Respect and Responsibility* (Bantam Books, 1994) by Thomas Lickona, a professor at Cortland State University New York.

84

Strategies infused from Thomas Lickona's book were crucial for our success. Especially important were Lickona's school-wide/classroom strategies and his "caring beyond the classroom" strategies. Dr. Lickona's comprehensive approach to character education calls upon the teacher to:

1. Be a caregiver, model and mentor; treat students with respect and care.
2. Create a moral community in the classroom by helping build positive relationships with and among students.
3. Practice moral discipline by helping students become self-disciplined and find alternative ways to handle anger.
4. Create a democratic classroom environment by giving students an opportunity to have input and to help the classroom and our school environment be safe and orderly.
5. Teach values through the curriculum and the daily operations of the school, including the special subjects of art, music, physical education, home economics, health, etc.

Any administrator who implements Lickona's comprehensive approach, and expects teachers to use the approach in their classrooms, should use the same principles in working with his or her staff. The administrator must be the leader, setting the example. I was very much conscious of this responsibility as we implemented the program.

To set an example for Lickona's first principle, "treating students with respect and care," I made it a priority to let staff know how much I respected and cared about them.

To create a moral community by helping build positive relationships, I asked the teachers to identify their students' talents and make use of them when appropriate. (This built on that exercise, described earlier, in which staff members recognized and shared their talents with each other.)

To model the third principle, "moral discipline by helping students become self-disciplined," we discussed how we would treat one another and model by example.

To support the fourth principle, "creating a democratic, orderly, and safe classroom environment," we worked together to make the entire school a safe and orderly environment for children to learn and adults to teach.

Lickona's fifth principle emphasizes integrating character education within the existing curriculum. We made sure that we would teach values through the curriculum and the daily operations of the school, including the special subjects like art and music. Working together, we integrated character education from the front office to the corridors to the cafeteria to the parking lot.

## The Dynamics of Success

Much of the success of our Ethical Citizenship and Courtesy Program could be traced to the commitment our staff made to improve the teaching and learning climate of our school. From that commitment flowed a sense of collective responsibility for the behavior and academic achievement of ALL our students.

The program provided explicit instruction in appropriate behaviors for a wide variety of situations, and it rewarded students for practicing those behaviors. The program also included recommendations from the county school district's ethical citizenship task force. All the values were taught as an integral part of the curriculum.

Our commitment to teach ethical citizenship included the commitment to act as positive role models for students. All staff worked at being responsible, courteous citizens not only in their interactions with each other, but in our interactions with students and parents. We expected students to respect themselves and others. Therefore, we treated students with respect. We wanted students to develop self-discipline. Therefore, we exercised self-discipline in our dealings with them and with our colleagues.

We built commitment from staff, parent, community and students to make this program a success. We knew that children model us and nothing happens with them immediately, but when they are surrounded by positive role models, change is sure to happen. Parents are very important to the character development of students. When children see their parents talking about—and trying to live by—the same values being discussed in school, you can achieve something close to a miracle.

A set of core values drove our efforts. Presentations of those values were made to the staff, parents, community and students. Integration of these values was an intrinsic part of the existing curriculum. In her reflections on life at Benjamin Foulois Academy, Janet Orben McMillan, the fifth and fourth grade teacher quoted earlier, summed it up this way:

> The character education program became a main strength that began to tie the whole community together. In turn, these students would take these values home—courage, self-discipline, and respect, among others.... The topics were discussed thoroughly and

used throughout literature, writing, role modeling, or wherever the staff could complement the topic. By focusing on character values one at a time, or weekly, students began to understand them and how that value could impact their life. Many of our students came from some pretty rough backgrounds, backgrounds with a lot of baggage. Often times, their home life didn't allow for teaching manners, determination, and responsibility. They focused on daily survival. As a staff, we felt compelled to nurture the character values because they would help our students lead better lives.

One additional, very important element contributed to our success. Staff development, training and attention to effective communication between all members of the staff kept us focused on our shared vision and improving the education of the BFTA students. Beyond any doubt, this focus and reinforcement of core virtues guided us and made a significant difference in the conduct and attitude of BFTA students and adults.

I was touched by a letter I received from Dawn Haley, a student who attended BFTA from kindergarten to 6th grade. Her letter, written during her senior year of high school, as she was filling out applications for college, gives all of us a perspective on how very, very important those first years of school are for a young person.

In the letter, she recalls how it felt to be "a three-foot-tall kindergartner surrounded by giant third and fourth graders." It was like being stuck in a "Jack and the Beanstalk fairy tale." She goes on to tell about how each of her teachers started her—and numerous other children—on the path to success. "My most remarkable memories," she wrote, "are the teachers, not the students... I think deeply about the stepping stones each teacher gave me to build my path of life. Can you imagine having the future of the world placed on your shoulders? God bless their souls! They spent six years with me in the same building, and that is why they stick with me in the long run. Middle school was too brief to get attached to my teachers, and in high school you are on your own."

Dawn emphasized how important the citizenship program was in shaping who she is today. "I do not question if I am ready for the real world, because I know my foundation is strong enough to deal with anything. An anonymous quote says, 'Success is not based on what you have, but who you are.' I know I can look in the mirror and honestly say to myself, 'I am successful,' and that is how I know I am."

As I close this section, I can't help but recall what was written on a photograph I received from a 6th grader who had just finished our school in June 1996. At our promotion exercise, her mother took a photograph of her daughter and me together. Later I received a copy of the snapshot. Alicia Hemphill had inscribed it, "You are a good principal, the teachers were great. It was just like being in a family."

## Leadership Insights

You don't have to be a teacher or administrator to start a character education program. Every time you make an ethical decision—sometimes this is hard to do—and let others know the basis for your action, you are educating for character. Every time you recognize someone for doing the right thing, you are reinforcing character education. There is a very simple motto, "There's no right way to do the wrong thing." That says it all.

# 11

## Character Education— More than a School Program

To educate a person in mind and not morals is to educate a menace to society.
—Theodore Roosevelt

Exactly what is this initiative called "character education" that has become such a huge topic of conversation? I define it as a way of life, a journey and not a destination. It's not a program; it's an ongoing process. It involves an organization's or group's stakeholders, those individuals who have a personal and abiding interest is seeing their group or organization become a healthy, life-affirming environment. In essence, it is a tacit agreement among all these stakeholders to practice the Golden Rule... "Do unto others as you wish others to do unto you."

That's it in a nutshell.

Think about the character traits that you admire in others, traits like respect, responsibility, caring, fairness, trustworthiness and citizenship. These traits are based on positive values (some writers prefer the word "virtues") that transcend all cultures, races, socioeconomic status and religious beliefs, and are listed in almost every character education "program." If you think about it, they are all extensions of the Golden Rule. When we treat others with respect, show care for their well-being, and take responsibility for our actions—with hope that we will be treated in like manner—we are practicing the Golden Rule.

Note that the definition of character education doesn't limit itself to something that happens in schools. Our experiences have shown how significant character education can be in creating safe, nurturing environments where teaching and learning thrive. These nurturing environments are not limited to classrooms; they exist in homes, workplaces, and communities. And some form of character education *should* be a part of those environments as well.

Can you imagine what life would be like if we all sincerely practiced The Golden Rule? I don't mean just *talking* about it, but *acting it out.* You see, it can be done. With hope, commitment, faith, dedication and courage it truly *can* be accomplished. It takes practice to do this. It must become a habit, just as many things we do become habits. Anything that you do over and over again becomes a habit, so why not start practicing the character traits that we wish to see in others?

The full benefits of character education in a school setting cannot be assessed immediately. As with most school reform initiatives, it will take three to five years before real results can be measured and evaluated. However, by performing formative and summative assessments, a school can obtain data and anecdotal evidence of positive changes. Also, long-term results will point toward improvements that have occurred not only in the social skills areas but also incrementally in academic achievement as well.

## Parenting with Character

Is it the school's responsibility to teach and develop character? This is a controversial question, one that is frequently raised. I would like to answer this question.

Many say character development is the job of the home. Yes, character development begins at home. Let me explain. Character development as it relates to the civic virtues that I have named is *learned* behavior, not something the infant is born with. Generally, young people do not necessarily do what adults *say* to do ... they do what they *see* us do. Any kindergarten teacher or first grade teacher could share a lot with you about that! So we must remember that we all are teachers of character, and that as parents or caregivers, we are the children's first teachers or leaders. As such, we lead at home by practicing and being role models or examples for children.

There is a quote attributed to comedian Danny Kay that says, "Children are like wet cement...whatever lands on them leaves an impression." Dorothy Law Nolte's poem, "Children Learn What They Live," expresses the same idea in a very powerful way. Most people are familiar with that poem. It starts by saying, "If children live with criticism, they learn to condemn " and goes on to talk about all the other emotions and attitudes that children absorb as a result of how we, as adults, interact with them: If children live with a sense of shame, they develop feelings of guilt. If they receive encouragement from the adults in their families, they learn to have self-confidence. And so on.

Several lines in the poem say more about character education in the home than I could ever express:

> If children live with sharing, they learn generosity.
> If children live with honesty, they learn truthfulness....
> If children live with kindness and consideration, they learn respect.

When we surround children with this kind of treatment, we are establishing attitudes and values that will last a lifetime. Qualities like generosity, truthfulness, and respect are just being "talked about"—*they are being lived!*

Several years ago, Dorothy Law Nolte and Rachel Harris revised the poem and expanded the ideas into a small book. For each line in the poem, they provide comments, anecdotes, and advice to parents to help them understand the full importance of each idea. (*Children Learn What They Live: Parenting to Inspire Values*, Workman Publishing, 1998). It's a beautiful little book—one that every parent should own!

## Sharing the Responsibility

Most people would agree that universal values such as those cited earlier should first be taught, modeled, practiced and recognized at home, especially by caregivers in their relationship with children, and among any siblings in their relationship with one another. We cannot always assume that this is happening! Parents should understand that they are teachers who are responsible for communicating the expectations and standards of integrity for their family. Most parents are performing this task, but their efforts need to be reinforced within and by the school, and within and by the community.

Students come to school from different experiences in character development. Some children have been taught verbally the important values (virtues) and their meanings. They have seen these values modeled by their parents, and their parents have encouraged them to practice those values. Other children come from homes where, for a variety of reasons, the adults have not made a conscious effort to talk about honesty, responsibility, and citizenship, nor have the adults made deliberate efforts to model these virtues for their children. A third group includes those children who have been taught by example that it is all right to be angry and fight, or to be dishonest, or even to steal.

Children from all three of these family community backgrounds arrive at our schools, where they begin a kindergarten through 12$^{th}$ grade experience with adults who serve as models for them. But that experience is only part of their lives. All children are influenced by what they experience in school, the home, the outside communities. Everything they see and hear has an effect on their behavior, as do the print and non-print media, the music industry, and a host of other experiences.

Let's not point fingers or start blaming everyone or everything—the parents, the schools, the media—when children misbehave. This kind of finger-pointing doesn't get us positive results.

Rather, we need to agree on universal values that can be reinforced from family to school to faith organizations to the greater community. Everyone wants to be respected and everyone would like for people to take responsibility for their actions and make decisions that will not be detrimental to either themselves or others.

Remember the words of Theodore Roosevelt, cited at the opening for this chapter, "To educate a person in mind and not morals is to educate a menace to society." We must educate the whole person. What would employers or society prefer: an individual with intellect, empathy and self-discipline, or a genius who doesn't care about other people and doesn't take responsibility for his or her actions? I believe that the first description is what we—in our roles as parents, relatives, employers, co-workers and members of society—desire.

In *Educating for Character*, Lickona defines character education as the intentional effort to teach young people to know the good, to desire the good and to do the good. I would expand that definition to include the word "adults." In many instances, it is not always only the children who need to know, care about and act upon these universal values. Adults need to be the role models and leaders.

So, yes, while character development begins at home, it is a shared responsibility of the home, school, faith organizations, neighborhood communities and society as a whole. Educating our young people to develop positive character traits depends on more than having a word of the week, displaying signs around the school, or 15 minutes of classroom instruction. The beginning of a character education program may be found in a kit or a book. But the process must be deeper and broader than that.

Sound character traits can be developed in young people only when the traits are taught to them, modeled for them and expected of them. Additionally, it is very important in this process that these young people be provided opportunities to practice the traits so as to demonstrate understanding and receive acknowledgement for their achievements. In schools, this process should always be accomplished within the context of teaching the existing curricula; i.e., social studies, language arts, physical education, etc. It should expand to include life experiences outside of school. It should not happen just in social studies, but also in social interactions in the neighborhood; not just in language arts, but in the language used to deal with friends and family; not just in physical education, but in the physical activities of work and play.

It doesn't happen 8 a.m. to 4 p.m. It is exercised from the time we wake up in the morning until we go to bed at night. It is exhibited at home with family, at work, in the faith communities and in the neighborhood. It's who we are individually and who we are as a society.

# 12

## Lessons for Leaders

*People do not follow programs, but leaders who inspire them.*
—John White

It was 5:00 p.m. on July 25, 1996, when I drove away from Benjamin Foulois Traditional Academy. As I looked back at the front of the school, a flood of emotions—sad and happy feelings all jumbled together—overcame me. I was saying goodbye to a staff of 85 enthusiastic, caring, committed, thoroughly professional human beings, all dedicated to being role models, mentors, and caretakers of children. I was leaving an attractive physical building where 821 children were developing into respectful, responsible young people who practiced empathy and self-discipline in their daily lives.

They had heard me say—twice, sometimes three times a week—that they had succeeded in making the school "a good place to be." As I recalled their faces, I caught a glimpse of the future. I could picture them as young adults, and later as adult members of their communities, each working to make a home, a neighborhood, a place of employment a *good place to be.* Moreover, the school would continue, in my absence, to prepare other children for a bright future.

During my final years at the Benjamin Foulois Traditional Academy, several questions hovered at the back of my mind. We had accomplished so much at the school. Could these accomplishments be replicated in other schools? More importantly, could the kind of caring community that evolved at this school be developed in organizations other than schools?

I know now that the answer to both questions is YES!

## You Can Make Your Organization "A Good Place To Be"

• Establish a shared vision within the community. Clearly articulate the vision and create a sense of where you're going. Visualize what you desire in your organization.

• Develop shared core values that all members can exhibit.

• Be an ethical leader: establish an ethical climate by modeling a standard of integrity that reflects your core values and that exhibits respect for others, responsibility, caring, honesty, fairness, trust, moral courage and flexibility. Be an example of what you expect in others.

• Motivate and inspire members of the community. Use motivational literature, stories and your personal history.

• Provide structure; be visible in your monitoring of activities and provide ongoing constructive feedback.

• Be positive, not negative.

• Learn how to control your anger.

• Respect and accept diversity.

• Be passionate, dedicated and committed to your purpose.

• *Make* service to the community *your primary goal; your goal is not your own advancement, not your personal agenda, and not your need to be the center of attraction. Help others maximize their potential. This is true leadership.*

• Walk the talk; live your message.

• Earn respect by giving it.

• Continue learning; don't be afraid to learn from others, including your subordinates. Establish a community of learners and leaders.

• Be empathic. Put yourself in the other person's shoes. Build on people's strengths.

• Be professional, and act professionally in everything you say and do.

• Encourage collegiality within the organizational community.

*continued on next page...*

Let me begin by telling you about Fort Foote Elementary School in Prince George's County, Maryland. During my last year at the Benjamin Foulois Traditional Academy, Robyn Zgorski, who had served as the Elementary Instructional Assistant (EIA), left to be a new principal at Fort Foote Elementary.

The cultural change we had experienced together at the Academy left a lasting impression on her. Before she left, she shared with me that she was going to use what she had learned. She was planning to implement components of our school's culture at her new school, and to use those components to support her *continued from previous page...*

• Include everyone, professionals as well as support positions. Communicate the idea that everyone is special. Don't thrive on titles.
• Organize your time; make more time for people and less for paper. Remember: people make programs work…not paper, not the program itself.
• Be open to the members of your community. Don't leave people wondering or unaware about what you are doing. Good leaders keep people aware of change before it happens.
• Be aware of who you are. Be in touch with your feelings, your character traits. Be aware of the verbal and nonverbal message you send to others as you interact with them.
• Have the courage to explore and to utilize the talents of all members within the community. Remember each of us has a talent.
• Treat everyone fairly. Don't show favoritism. Fairness is crucial; provide equity in resources, support and opportunities. Encourage everyone to reach his or her potential.
• Communicate expectations.
• Define and discuss roles and responsibilities.
• Build positive relationships among the people within the communities you are a part of.
• Establish a sense of community and a culture where others feel valued, cared about, appreciated and nurtured.
• Recognize both individuals and team efforts.
• Provide a means for communication, listening and allowing input from others. Allow for venting and do not take concerns personally.
• Empower others, have confidence, be secure and delegate responsibilities. Trust and give autonomy for others to do the work and carry out the mission.
• Provide training and professional development that is complementary to the purposes and goals of the organization.

individual vision of an ideal school. That vision included a very challenging goal: Fort Foote Elementary would become a Blue Ribbon School in five years.

I visited the school during the first to fifth years, and I could see Robyn's vision unfolding each year. Clearly, initiatives modeled after components at the Benjamin Foulois Academy were proving effective:
• Communications between administrators and staff, as well as among staff, became more open, thanks in part to the use of CHATS—Communicating Helps All Teachers Sessions.

• Employee of the Month and Feature Teacher initiatives helped staff members feel recognized and appreciated.

• The school's leaders surveyed teachers to determine their needs for training. These survey results were instrumental in shaping the direction and content of all staff development activities, which were ongoing. (Soliciting input from staff members and actually using it to benefit staff validates their efforts and demonstrates how much they are valued.)

• The school implemented an Ethical Citizenship and Courtesy Program similar to that used at the Academy—with similar results.

• The principal collaborated with the parents to make school uniforms required for the students.

At the end of the fifth year, the school's test scores had increased, discipline referrals and suspensions had decreased and parent involvement had become an important part of the school's culture. The school became not just a Blue Ribbon State School, but a *National* Blue Ribbon School!

How much credit for this should go to those programs modeled after our initiatives at the Benjamin Foulois Academy? To answer that question, remember that programs don't make changes happen—people do. Initiatives like CHATS and Ethical Citizenship Programs, along with the leadership of the principal and teachers and a strong and challenging curriculum, helped to establish a caring and supporting learning environment. *The people who worked in that environment made the changes happen.*

So, you see, caring communities such as those that evolved at the Benjamin Foulois Academy *can* be replicated. But we should not limit our visions of this possibility to schools. The transformation of a culture—the creation of a caring community—can happen in our homes, our faith organizations, our workplaces, our government organizations and our neighborhoods. It *will* happen if the leaders of each of these communities or organizations recapture the spirit of our fundamental values and traditional beliefs and adopt the concept that everyone is important and special. Everyone should have the opportunity to succeed regardless of race, religion, gender or socioeconomic status.

We must realize that children are our most important resource. The family, school, community and society must treat them as special. We must nurture, protect and care about them, their intellectual, physical, emotional and social health.... and *make the time* to do so.

## Lessons for Leaders: Home, School, Faith Organizations, Governments & Community

We are all in leadership positions at one time or another—as bosses or supervisors, as volunteers for civic, community, or faith-based organizations, and as parents. As a leader, you can make a difference. The boxed material in this chapter lists leadership principles that apply universally, to any organization. It's not the kind of leadership where a boss gives marching orders and makes sure everyone is standing in a straight line. Nor is it the kind of leadership where you become some kind of hero. Rather, it is leadership that nurtures and empowers others and prepares them for individual achievement and service to their communities.

As you review pages 96 and 97, think about the following key ideas. They are the essence of a service-based, empowering kind of leadership.

*Leadership starts with vision.* You must look within yourself and your spirit and know where you want to go, because if you don't know your purpose, it's impossible to go anywhere. Once you know where you want to go, picture what life will be like when you get there. Don't just daydream about it. Really picture it, in colorful detail. Believe that you can get there and take action to do so.

*Make your leadership value-based.* Identify a set of core values to guide you individually toward your vision. Model those values, and expect them to be modeled by all involved.

*Communicate your vision and values to all stakeholders in your organization.* Discuss the vision and values openly and incorporate them into everything that drives your organization. Unite your organization by asking its members to develop personal visions for each of their roles, based on values that align with and support the organization's vision and values.

*Empower individuals to achieve their maximum potential.* Expect that each person will become a professional in his or her role, regardless of what that role is. Provide the training and resources for professional growth. Help each person recognize his or her talents. Those talents are wings—give people freedom and opportunity to use those wings, to soar. Don't worry about where or how they will fly. Remember the geese. You will all soar as part of the same flock, guided by your shared vision and values.

*Provide time for effective communication and listening.* People need feedback, recognition and opportunity to talk through personal and professional issues. Create opportunities to dialogue professionally and to chat personally. You must have a *passion* for what you do, but also have *compassion* for others. Communicate your vision with passion, but listen to what each person has to say with compassion.

These elements—vision, values, communication, empowerment, and listening—work together. They establish a sense of community, belonging and connectedness.

If you're a parent, think about how these principles apply to the structure of your home and to raising and teaching your children. If you are a supervisor, think about how you can apply these components within your organization. If you are in government or serve as a political leader, ask what you can reflect on, build on or change as you lead. If you are a member of a faith organization, ask how you can help the adults and children in  your faith community practice good citizenship throughout their daily lives.

Always think of yourself as performing a service to help prepare others for individual or community achievement. It is only then that we will have a more civil society where respect and responsibility become a way of life.

# About the Author

## Mary Curtis Aranha

Mary Curtis Aranha is currently Director of Character Education at the Maryland State Department of Education. She is recognized nationally as a practitioner, catalyst and visionary leader in education and instructional leadership. As a keynote speaker and workshop leader at professional conferences, she often tells the story of the changes that occurred at the Benjamin Foulois Traditional Academy during her term as principal. The lessons that she and her staff learned during that school's transformation have had a positive influence on thousands of teachers and administrators across America.

Mary has more than thirty years of experience as a professional educator, on levels ranging from Head Start programs to adult education. She teaches graduate courses at Trinity College and has taught inmates of the District of Columbia Department of Corrections.

The character education process implemented at the Benjamin Foulois Academy received widespread recognition for its success in addressing Goal 3 of the America 200 (Youth Violence) initiative. Specifically, recognition for this program came from the Washington, DC, Metropolitan Area Council of Governments, the Prince George's County Board of Education, and the Maryland Center for Character Education. Mary also received a proclamation from the Governor of Maryland for her outstanding work on the Governor's Citizenship Subcommittee on Youth, Citizenship, and Violence Prevention. She served as a participant/panelist at the 1997 White House Communitarians Network Conference on Character Education. She was selected by American Mothers, Inc., as Maryland's 1999 State Mother of the Year.

She is the author of various professional articles and the featured presenter in the video, *Leadership: The Character Education Imperative.*

# ADDITIONAL MATERIALS PUBLISHED/PRODUCED BY NATIONAL PROFESSIONAL RESOURCES, INC.

*Character Education Connections: For School, Home & Community - A Guide for Integrating Character Education*

Diane Stirling, Georgia Archibald, Linda McKay and Shelley Berg

This is a clear, concise, holistic resource for classroom teachers with a thoughtful collection of approaches to integrating character education into daily learning and school life. Well-written and organized, it provides an excellent overview of the field with a wealth of specific, field-tested plans for every level from K – 12.
2002, soft cover, 344 pages
Order #CECA-AGPT                    $39.95

*Character and Coaching: Building Virtue in Athletic Programs*

John M. Yeager, Amy L. Baltzell, John N. Buxton, & Wallace B. Bzdell

This book is written **for** coaches **by** coaches. The authors are affiliated with the Center for the Advancement of Ethics and Character, a recognized leader of Character Education in the United States. Their collective experience - as athletes, coaches, and program directors from all levels, youth programs to professional athletics - creates a resource with a depth and practicality that sets it apart from other works in the field.
2001, soft cover, 194 pages
Order # CHCO-AGPT            $24.95

*The Power of Social Skills in Character Development: Helping Diverse Learners Succeed*

Jennifer L. Scully

This book gives you 80 powerful, classroom-tested lesson plans. A complete program for helping your students gain self-esteem and improve relationships with peers, teachers and adults outside of school.
2000, soft cover, 198 pages
Order # PSSC-AGPT                    $29.95

*Character Kaleidoscope: A Practical, Standards-Based Resource Guide for Character Development*

Mirka Christensen with Susan Wasilewski

A resource filled with detailed, practical ideas for bringing character into the classroom. All of the strategies are standards-based and easy to integrate into any curriculum.
2000, soft cover, 152 pages
Order # CHKA-AGPT                    $29.95

*Engaging the Resistant Child Through Computers: A Manual to Facilitate Social & Emotional Learning*

Maurice J. Elias, Ph.D., Brian S. Friedlander, Ph.D. & Steven E. Tobias, Psy.D.

This book is written for practicing clinicians, school psychologists, social workers, guidance counselors, teachers, and others who work with children (preschoolers through adolescence).
2001, soft cover, 185 pages
Order # UCER-AGPT                    $39.95

## Leadership: The Character Education Imperative

*Mary Curtis Aranha, Director of Character Education, Division of Instruction & Staff Development, Maryland State Dept. of Education*

Given rising incidence of discipline problems and declining parental involvement in the moral development of their children, schools and agencies are faced with increased need for leadership that incorporated character education as an essential component of their programs. Additionally the aftermath of violence in the schools has resulted in a nation refocused on the role of leadership in the development of a school climate that is safe: one based on core virtues that promote individual character development. No longer can effective leadership be defined solely in terms of competence, organizational structure and management skills. Rather it must include a commitment to the demonstration of sound character by all members of the learning community, creating an environment built on virtues like mutual respect and responsibility. Mary Aranha, utilizing her classroom as well as administrative experience, presents a compelling argument for the role of leadership in character development.

2000, VHS, 36 minutes          Order #VLEA-AGPT          $99.95

### Character Education: Application in the Classroom

These videos provide educators with replicable ideas on how to integrate Character Education into existing classroom activities and to create a moral culture in the school community.

Elementary, 42 min.      Order #VCEE-AGPT          $89.95
Spanish subtitles        Order# VCEESP-AGPT        $99.95
Secondary, 40 min.       Order #VCES-AGPT          $89.95
Spanish subtitles        Order #VCESSP-AGPT        $99.95
Also available in PAL format

### Character Education: Restoring Respect and Responsibility in our Schools

*Thomas Lickona*

Thomas Lickona, a recognized leader in the Character Education movement, presents an insightful and compelling argument for the role of schools in the development of student respect, responsibility, and moral education.

VHS, 44 min.      Order #VCED-AGPT   $79.95
Spanish subtitles   Order # VCESP-AGPT $89.95
Also available in PAL format

### Eleven Principles of Effective Character Education

*Thomas Lickona and Catherine Lewis*

Commissioned by the Character Education Partnership, (CEP) the *Eleven Principles of Effective Character Education* presents a comprehensive guide to the development and assessment of character education programs in our nation's schools.

VHS, 40 min.      Order #VEPC-AGPT   $89.95
Also available in PAL format

Order from: National Professional Resources, Inc., 25 South Regent Street, Port Chester, NY 10573. Tel - 1-800-453-7461, Fax - 914-937-9327. www.nprinc.com. Shipping & Handling: $5 per item.

# RESOURCES AVAILABLE FROM
## *NATIONAL PROFESSIONAL RESOURCES, INC.*
## (BOOKS & VIDEOS)

Abourjilie, Charlie. *Developing Character For Classroom Success.* Chapel Hill, NC: Character Development Publishing, 2000. $12.00

Adderholdt, Miriam. & Goldberg, Jan. *Perfectionism: What's Bad About Being Too Good?* Minneapolis, MN: Free Spirit Publishing, 1999. $12.95

Beane, Allan L. The Bully Free Classroom: *Over 100 Tips and Strategies for Teachers K-8.* Minneapolis, MN: Free Spirit Publishing, 1999. $19.95

Beedy, Jeffrey. *Sports Plus: Developing Youth Sports Programs that Teach Positive Values.* Hamilton, MA: Project Adventure, Inc., 1997. $16.00

Begun, Ruth W. *Ready-to-Use Social Skills Lesson (4 levels: Pre K-K; 1-3; 4-6; 7-12)* West Nyack, NY: Center for Applied Research, 1995. $29.95 each

Bennett, William J. *Book of Virtues.* New York, NY: Simon & Schuster, 1996. $16.00

Bennett, William J. *Moral Compass.* New York, NY: Simon & Schuster, 1996. $16.00

Benson, Peter L., Galbraith, Judy, & Espeland, Pamela. *What Teens Need To Succeed.* Minneapolis, MN: Free Spirit Press, 1998. $14.95

Berman, Sally. *Service Learning for the Multiple Intelligences Classroom.* Arlington Heights, VA: Skylight, 1999. $34.95

Bernardo, Rudy, et al. *Building Character Schoolwide: Creating a Caring Community in Your School.* Chapel Hill, NC Character Development Publishing, 2000. $18.00

Bocchino, Rob. *Emotional Literacy: To Be a Different Kind of Smart.* Thousand Oaks, CA: Corwin Press, 1999. $24.95

Boston University School of Education (Editor). *The Art of Loving Well*. Boston, MA: 1995. $19.95

Brooks, B. David & Goble, Frank. *Case for Character Education*. Northridge, CA: Studio Four Productions, 1997. $11.95

Canfield, Jack & Hansen, Mark V. *Chicken Soup for the Kid's Soul: 101 Stories of Courage, Hope & Laughter.* Deerfield Beach, FL: Health Communications, Inc., 1998. $12.95

*Character Connections Monthly Newsletter*. National Professional Resources, Inc . (Publisher). $99.00 yearly subscription

Caroll, Jeri A. Gladhart, Marsha A. & Petersen, Dixie L. C*haracter Building/Literature-Based Theme*. Carthage, IL: Teaching & Learning Company, 1997. $14.95

Cohen, Jonathan. *Educating Minds & Hearts*. New York, NY: Teacher's College Press, 1999. $21.95

Coles, Robert. *Moral Intelligence of Children*. New York, NY: Random House, Inc., 1997. $21.00

Delisle, Jim. *Growing Good Kids*. Minneapolis, MN: Free Spirit Publishing, 1996. $21.95

DeRoche, Edward F. & Williams, Mary M. *Educating Hearts & Minds.* Thousand Oaks, CA: Corwin Press, 1998. $22.95

Dotson, Anne C., & Dotson, Karen D. *Teaching Character/Parent's Guide*. Chapel Hill, NC: Character Development Publishing, 1997. $12.00

Dotson, Anne C., & Dotson, Karen D. *Teaching Character/Teacher's Guide*. Chapel Hill, NC: Character Development Publishing, 1997. $24.95

Elias, Maurice. *Raising Emotionally Intelligent Teenagers: Parenting with Love, Laughter and Limits*. New York, NY: Three Rivers Press, 1999. $24.00

Elias, Maurice, et al. *Promoting Social-Emotional Learning: Guidelines for Educators.* Alexandria, VA: ASCD, 1997. $22.95

Elias, Maurice, & Tobias, Steven. Social Problem Solving: Interventions in the Schools. New York, NY: Guilford Press, 1996.

Espeland, Pamela & Verdick, Elizabeth. *Making Every Day Count: Daily Readings for Young People on Solving Problems, Setting Goals & Feeling Good About Yourself.* Minneapolis, MN: Free Spirit Publishing, 1998. $9.95

Espeland, Pamela & Wallner, Rosemary. *Making the Most of Today: Daily Readings for Young People on Self-Awareness, Creativity & Self-Esteem.* Minneapolis, MN: Free Spirit Publishing, 1998. $9.95

Etzioni, Amit. New Golden Rule: *Community & Morality.* New York, NY: Basic Books, 1996. $27.50

Garbarino, James. *Lost Boys.* New York, NY: The Free Press, 1999. $25.00

Garbarino, James. *Raising Children in a Socially Toxic Environment.* San Francisco, CA: Jossey-Bass, 1995. $27.95

Girard, Kathryn & Koch, Susan J. *Conflict Resolution in the Schools: A Manual for Educators.* San Francisco, CA: Jossey-Bass, 1996. $35.00

Glasser, William. *Building A Quality School: A Matter of Responsibility* (Video). National Professional Resources, Inc., 1998. $99.00

Glasser, William. *Choice Theory.* New York, NY: Harper Collins, 1998. $23.00

Glasser, William. T*he Quality School: Managing Students Without Coercion.* New York, NY: Harper Collins, 1990. $12.00

Glenn, H. Stephen, *Raising Self-Reliant Children in a Self-Indulgent World.* Orem, UT: Empowering People, 1989. $12.95

Glenn, H. Stephen. *Seven Strategies for Developing Capable Students.* Orem, UT: Empowering People, 1998. $14.95

Goleman, Daniel. *Emotional Intelligence: Why It Can Matter More Than IQ*. New York, NY: Bantam Books, 1995. $13.95

Goleman, Daniel. *Emotional Intelligence: A New Vision For Educators* (Video). National Professional Resources, Inc., 1996. $89.95

Harris, Pat, et al. *Character Education: Application in the Classroom, Secondary Edition* (Video). National Professional Resources, Inc., 1998. $89.95

Healy, Jane M. *Failure to Connect*. New York, NY: Simon & Schuster, 1998. $25.00

Hillman, James. *Soul's Code*. New York, NY: Random House, 1996. $23.00

Hoffman, Judith B. & Lee, Anne R. *Character Education Workbook: For School Boards, Administrators & Community Leaders*. Chapel Hill, NC: Character Development Publishing, 1997. $12.00

Josephson, Michael & & Hanson, Wes. *Power of Character: Prominent Americans Talk About Life, Family, Work, Values & More*. San Francisco, CA: Jossey-Bass, 1998. $23.50

Kagan, Miguel et al. *Classbuilding*. San Clemente, CA: Kagan Cooperative Learning, 1995. $25.00

Kagan, Laurie, et al. *Teambuilding*. San Clemente, CA: Kagan Cooperative Learning, 1997. $25.00

Kagan, Spencer. *Building Character Through Cooperative Learning* (Video). National Professional Resources, Inc., 1999. $99.95

Kendall, John S. & Marzano, Robert J. *Content Knowledge K-12 Standards, Second Edition*. Aurora, CO: Mid-continent Regional Educational Laboratory, Inc., 1997. $47.95

Kidder, Rushworth W. *How Good People Make Tough Choices: Resolving the Dilemmas for Ethical Living*. New York, NY: William Morrow Company, Inc. 1995. $11.00

Kilpatrick, William and Gregory, & Wolf, Suzanne M. *Books That Build Character: A Guide to Teaching Your Child Moral Values Through Stories*. New York, NY: Touchstone, 1994. $11.00

Kohn, Alfie. *Punished By Rewards*. New York, NY: Houghton Mifflin Co., 1993. $13.95

Kohn, Alfie. *What to Look for in a Classroom: And Other Essays*. San Francisco, CA: Jossey-Bass, 1998. $25.00

Krovetz, Martin L. *Fostering Resiliency: Expecting All Students to Use Their Minds and Hearts Well*. Thousand Oaks, CA: Corwin Press, 1999. $24.95

Lewis, Barbara A. *Kid's Guide to Service Projects*. Minneapolis, MN: Free Spirit Publishing, 1995. $10.95

Lewis, Barbara A. *Kid's Guide to Social Action*. Minneapolis, MN: Free Spirit Publishing, 1998. $16.95

Lewis, Barbara A. *What Do You Stand For? A Kid's Guide to Building Character*. Minneapolis, MN: Free Spirit Publishing, 1997. $18.95

Lewis, Catherine, et al. *Eleven Principles of Effective Character Education* (Video). National Professional Resources, Inc., 1997. $89.95

Lickona, Thomas et al. *Character Education: Restoring Respect & Responsibility in Our Schools* (Video). National Professional Resources, Inc., 1996. $79.95

Lickona, Thomas. *Educating for Character: How our Schools can Teach Respect & Responsibility*. New York, NY: Bantam Books, 1992. $14.95

Lickona, Thomas. *Raising Good Children*. New York, NY: Bantam Books, 1994. $13.95

Live Wire Media (Publisher). *Character Way Learning Program* (3 module set), 1995. $399.00

Live Wire Media (Publisher). *In Search of Character* (10 video set). $649.

Lockwood, Anne T. *Character Education: Controversy & Consensus.* Thousand Oaks, CA: Corwin Press, 1997. $12.95

Macan, Lynn, et al. *Character Education: Application in the Classroom, Elementary Edition* (Video). National Professional Resources, Inc., 1998. $89.95

The MASTER Teacher, Inc. (Publisher). *Lesson Plans for Character Education, Elementary Edition.* Manhattan, KS: 1998. $59.95

The MASTER Teacher, Inc. (Publisher). *Lesson Plans for Character Education, Secondary Edition.* Manhattan, KS: 1998. $59.95

McCourt, Lisa. *Chicken Soup for Little Souls* (7 book set). Deerfield Beach, FL: Health Communications, Inc., 1998. $99.95

McKay, Linda et al. *Service Learning: Curriculum, Standards and the Community* (Video), National Professional Resources, Inc., 1998. $99.00

Murphy, Madonna M. *Character Education in America's Blue Ribbon Schools.* Lancaster, PA: Technomic Publishing, 1997. $44.95

Nelson, Jane. *Positive Discipline.* Orem, UT: Empowering People, 1996. $11.00

Packer, Alex J. *How Rude! The Teenagers' Guide to Good Manners, Proper Behavior, and Not Grossing People Out.* Minneapolis, MN: Free Spirit Publishing, 1997. $19.95

Perlstein, Ruth & Thrall, Gloria. *Ready-to-Use Conflict Resolution Activities for Secondary Students.* West Nyack, NY: Center for Applied Research in Education, 1996. $29.95

Pert, Candace. *Emotion: Gatekeeper to Performance – The Mind/Body Connection* (Video). National Professional Resources, Inc., 1999. $99.00

Pert, Candace. *Molecules of Emotion.* New York, NY: Simon & Schuster, 1999. $14.00

Pipher, Mary. *Shelter of Each Other: Rebuilding Our Families.* New York, NY: Ballantine Books, 1997. $12.95

Pollack, William. *Real Boys.* New York, NY: Henry Holt & Co., 1999. $13.95

Renzulli, Joseph. *Developing the Gifts & Talents of ALL Students* (Video), National Professional Resources, Inc., 1999. $99.95

Romain, Trevor. *Cliques, Phonies, & Other Baloney.* Minneapolis, MN: Free Spirit Publishing, 1998. $9.95

Rusnak, Timothy. *Integrated Approach to Character Education.* Thousand Oaks, CA: Corwin Press, 1998. $21.95

Ryan, Devin A. & Bohlin, Karen E. *Building Character in Schools.* San Francisco, CA: Jossey-Bass, 1998. $25.00

Sadlow, Sarah. *Advisor/Advisee Character Education.* Chapel Hill, NC: Character Development Publishing, 1998. $24.95

Salovey, Peter et al. *Optimizing Intelligences: Thinking, Emotion & Creativity* (Video). National Professional Resources, Inc., 1998. $99.95

Sapon-Shevin, Mara. *Because We Can Change The World: A Practical Guide to Building Cooperative, Inclusive Classroom Communities.* Needham Heights, MA: Allyn & Bacon, 1999. $29.95

Sergiovanni, Thomas J. *Leadership for the Schoolhouse.* San Francisco, CA: Jossey-Bass, 1996. $29.95

Sergiovanni, Thomas J. *Moral Leadership: Getting to the Heart of School Improvement.* San Francisco, CA: Jossey-Bass, 1992. $34.95

Shure, Myrna B. *Raising a Thinking Child.* New York, NY: Henry Holt & Co., Inc., 1994. $12.00

Shure, Myrna B. *Raising a Thinking Pre-Teen.* New York, NY: Henry Holt & Co., Inc., 2000. $23.00

Sizer, Ted. *Crafting of America's Schools* (Video), National Professional Resources, Inc., 1997. $99.95

Soder, Roger. *Democracy, Education and the Schools.* San Francisco, CA: Jossey-Bass, 1996. $32.95

Stirling, Diane, Archibald, Georgia, McKay, Linda & Berg, Shelley. *Character Education Connections for School, Home and Community.* Port Chester, NY: National Professional Resources, Inc., 2002. $39.95

Teolis, Beth. *Ready-to-Use: Conflict Resolution Activities, Elementary Edition.* West Nyack, NY: Center for Applied Research in Education, 1998. $29.95

Urban, Hal. *Life's Greatest Lessons: 20 Things I Want My Kids to Know.* Redwood City, CA: Great Lessons Press, 1992. $14.00

Vincent, Philip F. *Developing Character in Students.* Chapel Hill, NC: New View Publications, 1994. $12.95

Vincent, Philip F. *Promising Practices in Character Education: Nine Success Stories from Across the Country, Volume II.* Chapel Hill, NC: Character Development Publishing, 1999. $14.00

Vincent, Philip F. *Rules & Procedures for Character Education.* Chapel Hill, NC: Character Development Group, 1998. $14.00

Wiley, Lori Sandford. *Comprehensive Character-Building Classroom.* DeBary, FL: Longwood Communications, 1998. $19.95

# Notes